"Cheerful, matter of fact information and full of common sense, useful for parents as well as girls and boys."

Fionnuala Kilfeather
National Parents Council Primary

"The author, a teacher with wide experience of sex instruction, has done an excellent job in bringing plenty of useful information to an age group that often has difficulty in understanding it".

Irish Farmer's Journal

"This book would be ideal reading for girls and boys approaching the age of puberty, and would provide useful resource for teachers or parents in the provision of sex education for children".

Education Today

"A simple, practical and amusing book for any teacher or parent to use, making an awkward subject a lot easier to address".

Primary Times

Girlfacts

By cathy Bee

Everything you ever wanted to know about a lot of stuff

Edited by Aidan Herron

POOLBEG

This edition 2006

Published 1995
by Poolbeg Press Ltd
123 Grange Hill, Baldoyle
Dublin 13, Ireland
E-mail: poolbeg@poolbeg.com

3 5 7 9 10 8 6 4

A catalogue record for this book is available from the British Library.

ISBN 1-85371-504-2
ISBN 978 1 85371 504 4 (From January 2007)

Illustrations by Adrienne Geoghegan
Cover design and setting by Poolbeg Press Ltd.
Printing by Litografia Roses, Spain

www.poolbeg.com

To Amy, my best critic

contents

Foreword . . .

Hi! Welcome to *Girlfacts*.

This is the girls' side of the book and it's full of facts.

That's why it's called *Girlfacts*.

I know it's obvious, but I just thought I'd point it out to you.

Message for Boys

If you're a boy (check with your parents if you're not sure), go to the OTHER SIDE OF THE BOOK. That's where you'll find Boyfacts. Leave this side to the girls.

(End of Message for Boys)

In *Girlfacts*, you'll read about all the changes that happen to human beings as they develop from tiny babies to adulthood.

And Cathy will also tell you lots of other things about growing up which you'll need to know as you get older.

When you've read *Girlfacts* (and *Boyfacts* – but don't let on), you'll know more about babies, puberty and sex than your parents do. But don't be mean with this information. It's possible your parents will need to be told the *facts of life* as well, and if they don't hear them from you, their daughter, then who do you think will tell them? So make sure to have a good chat with them soon.

I hope you enjoy reading *Girlfact*s.

The Editor.

(Hey! You, boy. I thought you were told to flip the book over. Oh, all right, then. But I hope you're a fast reader.)

One
Nice to Meet You

Hi, my name's Cathy Bee.

I'm glad you're reading this book with me. I have lots of things to tell you and I know that you'll have plenty of questions for me. When you talk to me, *you can use this kind of print.* Okay? Good, that's settled then.

Before we begin, we should double-check our Girl Security System. It'll just take a moment.

SECURITY CHECKPOINT

(Do you look like this:)

GIRL

BOY

If the answer is yes, it's okay to read on.
(But if you look like this:)

. . . you're in big trouble. Do you know why?

Because this part of the book is for girls and we don't take kindly to guys who stick their noses in where they're not wanted. So go back to your own end of the book.

(End of Security Check)

That's telling them, isn't it?

Good. We're on our own now.

I thought we might have to be rude there to get rid of them. It's nice to be on our own for a while.

And it's also nice to be able to discuss sex and the way our bodies develop without having to listen to boys butting in all the time. You could tell them things a hundred times and still they wouldn't have a clue what you're talking about. It's not their fault that they're so immature. It's just that they're boys.

Before you read any more, put a sign saying:

"Do not disturb for at least six hours"

on your door. Then make yourself nice and cosy in your favourite soft chair. Fluff up that cushion behind your back and relax into a comfy reading position. The notice on the door should keep everyone away for a while.

Now you can read on in peace.

Remembering Pink

Do you remember when nearly everything you had was pink?

No.

Well, when you were born, your mother and father told everyone immediately that you were a girl.

So what did everybody in your family do? They descended on the hospital with loads of pink things.

- Pink babygrows
- Pink dribblers
- Pink elephants. Pink rabbits. Pink Panthers
- Pink blankets
- Pink soothers
- Pink socks

Pink, pink and more pink.

And what happened when you went home?

A pink room – that's what!

Pink walls. Pink curtains. Pink carpet. Pink cot.

No wonder we screamed so much when we were babies. We wanted a little more variety when it came to colour. Mind you, it's just as bad for boys. They had to put up with blue.

Maybe pink's not so bad after all . . .

But this book isn't about colour, is it?

Supposing pink and blue were banned from hospitals, how would people know whether babies were girls or boys?

That's easy. They'd look at their private parts.

Very good.

But what happens when you want to find out more about the private parts of our bodies and how they work? People can be very shy when it comes to talking about these things.

I'm not shy.

Good. Then perhaps it's a good time to talk about sex, and babies, and how our bodies develop. And I'll also tell you about how boys develop. Now, where do you want me to begin?

Tell me about periods first.

Ah, that's where most girls like to begin. All right, let's talk about periods.

(New chapter, please.)

Two
Menstruation

You've probably heard some things about **periods** already, but I'm going to tell you a lot more about them.

If at any stage you don't understand what I'm telling you, stop and go back over it again. It's important to understand everything properly.

First of all, I'd like you to meet your body.

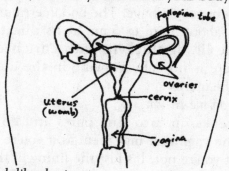

I don't look like that!

Yes, you do. On the inside. That's where the private parts of a girl's body are. A girl's genital area is called the **vulva**.

Look at the illustration carefully.

The **ovaries** are connected to the **uterus (womb)** by the **Fallopian tubes**. There are two ovaries, one on either side of the uterus.

The **cervix** is the name for the entrance to the uterus.

The **vagina** is the opening between your legs which leads to the uterus.

Urine (pee) comes out through the **urethra** at the bottom of the vagina.

You can see that all these body parts are connected. And I'm sure you know that the uterus, or womb, is the special place in a woman's body where a baby grows until it is ready to be born.

Of course I know that. Tell me something I don't know.

All right. The lining, or wall, of the uterus is called the **endometrium**.

I've never heard that word before.

Not many people have. The endometrium is really very thin, about 3mm to 5mm at its thickest. Each month the lining thickens with enriched blood. When there is no baby growing in the uterus, the lining of the uterus . . .

The en-do-me-tri-um

. . . breaks up into tiny parts and comes out through the vagina. It may seem as if you're bleeding but in fact you're not. It's just the lining of the uterus disintegrating and mixing with a small quantity of blood to carry it away.

And that's called a period?

Yes, that's all there is to it.

How often does this happen?

At the start, your periods won't come at regular intervals but as you become older and your periods fall into a regular pattern, they will occur roughly every 28 days. After a while, every girl gets to know her own monthly cycle.

Why are periods also called Menstruation?

Because it comes from the Latin word "mensis" meaning "month". Menstruation occurs approximately every twenty-eight days or once a month.

And do all women get periods?

If they're healthy, this happens to every woman in the world. Once they get to the age when their bodies begin to develop, their periods begin.

What exactly happens during the four weeks?

Good question. I've included an illustration to help you understand this part. I know it looks complicated but we'll go through it week by week to see what happens.

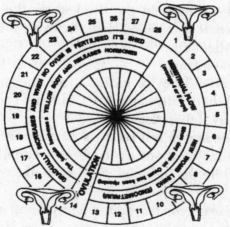

The menstrual cycle

LET'S START WITH DAY 1: Can you see that in the illustration? That marks the beginning of the first week.

The period begins when a small quantity of blood,

11

carrying the disintegrated endometrium with it, trickles out through the vagina. This discharge can last from approximately three to six days but the amount of blood that comes out is not very significant.

At the same time, an ovum in one of the ovaries begins to ripen.

IN THE SECOND WEEK: The ovum continues to mature and rises towards the surface of the ovary. Meanwhile the lining of the uterus . . .

The end-o-me-tri-um

. . . That's right . . . starts to thicken again as it fills with rich blood cells.

BY DAY 14: Or early in the third week, the ovum is now mature. It is expelled from the ovary and moves into the Fallopian tube.

What a weird name.

Not really. They're called after the man who discovered them. His name was Gabriello Fallopius, a 16th century Italian doctor.

It still sounds weird. What are these tubes like?

Well, they're about as thick as a pencil on the outside, while the inside of the tube is like where the lead is.

And the ovum can move down a tiny tunnel like that?

Yes, the ovum keeps on travelling down the Fallopian tube until it gets to the uterus. This is called **ovulation**.

The uterus and womb are the same, aren't they?

Yes. Well, in this third week the endometrium

becomes softer because it's getting ready to receive a **fertilised ovum**.

What's that?

Just let me finish with menstruation first.

IN THE FOURTH WEEK: If the ovum has not been fertilised, the lining breaks away from the uterus and disintegrates. This is because the lining is not needed to nurture a baby.

What happens is this: the endometrium breaks up into tiny pieces and is shed along with blood cells as the period discharge.

This comes out through the vagina.

But what happens to the ovum?

The unfertilised ovum passes out too, but because it's so small it's not noticeable.

You are now at day 28 in the illustration, the end of the period. It's now time for a new period to begin. Back to day 1 and the whole cycle starts off all over again.

Wow! And to think that this happens to every woman in the world!

Yes. So you see, when you start your periods, you won't be the only one. Most girls begin to menstruate by the age of eleven or twelve, but don't worry if it hasn't happened to you yet. I was fourteen when I started my periods. It's even possible for some girls to begin before they're eleven. Others may have to wait a little longer. It's different for every girl. But the important thing is that you'll start your periods at a time that's right for you.

Here's a close-up of what the outside of your genital area looks like.

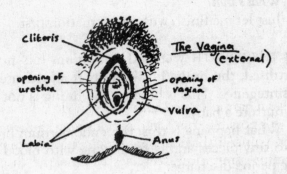

The **labia** are the folds of skin covering the entrance to the vagina, while the **clitoris** looks like a small bump just above the urethra.

Now, I know you're bursting with questions.

Yeah, I've lots of things to ask.

Then we'll have to start a new chapter.

(New chapter, please.)

Three
More Facts about Menstruation

Does it hurt when you have your period?

It's possible that some periods may cause you aches and pains. If that happens, you could try some gentle tummy-stretching exercises to ease the discomfort. Perhaps sitting with your knees up holding a hot water bottle to your tummy, or taking a warm bath, might also help. Whatever happens, make sure to tell your father or mother if you have any discomfort at all, so that they can decide what's the best thing for you to do.

Will people know when I have my period? I'd die of embarrassment if anyone found out.

Lots of girls feel like that. No, there's no way for people to know whether or not you've started your periods. Nobody will see any difference in you at all. So it'll be your own private business unless you decide to tell someone.

Of course, when you get your first one, you should tell your mother and father immediately. It's important for them to know because it's a sign that you've become a young woman.

After that, you can decide who else should know.

Should boys know about periods?

Yes, of course they should. Actually, Peter has told

boys about menstruation in *Boyfacts*. After all, boys shouldn't be left in ignorance.

How much blood is lost during menstruation?

Not a lot. Only about two tablespoonfuls in all. It just seems like a lot more.

Do women have periods all their lives?

No. Periods stop when women reach middle-age. This is called the **menopause**. After the menopause, women can no longer have any babies.

Is the period discharge always the same?

No, some days the discharge may be heavier than others. It may start slowly, become heavier, then gradually go away. It's also possible that one period may be heavier than the next. Or that they may not come on time every month. It's different for every woman. But don't worry. In time, you'll get to know your own individual cycle.

It's important to tell your mother or father if you notice any change in your periods. I know your mother knows much more about them than your father, but what would you do if you were concerned about something and your mother wasn't around? Then you'd have to tell your father or perhaps your big sister. If you were in school you might tell an approachable teacher. If you're ever worried about your periods, tell a responsible person immediately.

What do you do to catch the bleeding?

I'm sure you've seen advertisements on television for **sanitary protection**. This comes as either **tampons** or as **sanitary towels**. Both are **disposable** – that means they are disposed of after use. The sanitary towel is a pad of absorbent material that fits comfortably between the legs.

PAD

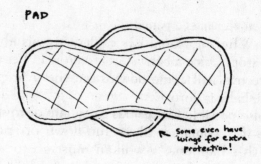

Some even have
wings for extra
protection!

The tampon is a small wad of tightly packed cotton. It is placed inside the vagina and it fits so snugly that you won't even know that you're wearing it. A tampon absorbs the discharge before it can come out of the vagina.

TAMPON

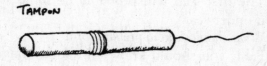

Ask your mother to show you a tampon and a pad. Talk to her about which you should use. Try out both methods and see which you prefer. If you have a big sister, ask her which she uses. I'm sure you'll find her advice useful as well.

Does a tampon ever get stuck?

No, because there's a string firmly attached to it which remains outside the vagina. That's there to help you pull it out.

17

Can it go up too far, say, into the womb?

No.

Do you ever miss a period?

Yes. When a woman is expecting a baby, her periods stop. Once a baby starts to grow in her womb, no more ova will come down from the ovaries until after the baby is born.

It's also possible for periods to be late or to stop for a while if a woman is ill, or run-down or anorexic. When this happens, a woman must go to see her doctor immediately.

Could you get your first period in school or on the bus?

There's no knowing where you'll be when you first begin your periods. And you won't know the exact time that the discharge will begin so it's wise to be prepared for it.

How will I know when my first period comes?

The first sign will probably be some staining on your underwear.

What should I do to prepare for it?

First, you should know all about what exactly is going to happen when your period starts so that you won't be worried or get a fright.

Then, you should start to carry some form of sanitary protection around with you in case you begin your periods when you're out of the house. This is something you can do without any fuss. Decide with your mother, or an older sister, or a close friend, what kind of sanitary protection is most suitable for you.

Will I be teased if I'm last to begin my periods?

Every girl changes into a young woman at a certain stage in her life. It just happens at a different time for each individual. If one girl begins her periods earlier than her friends, it gives her no right to tease others about it. After all, it's not something we can control.

Periods begin at a time that's right for each person, so teasing is out.

My friends are always talking about periods. Is that okay?

Yes, there's nothing wrong with that, as long as the information being passed around is correct and accurate. The best thing to do is to tell your mother and father what's being said so that you can check out whether it's right or not. Some girls exaggerate quite a lot so you have to be careful not to believe all that you hear.

What's a fertilised ovum?

Ah. I must have answered all your questions about menstruation if you now want to find out about the fertilised ovum.

Tell you what. Let's talk about the fertilised ovum in a new chapter. Do you want to rest for a while? You look a bit exhausted after all that talk about periods.

No. I want to go on.

Well, the next chapter is quite long and there's a lot more serious stuff in it.

Can I say it this time?

Say what?

New chapter, please.

If you want to.

NEW CHAPTER, PLEASE!

Oh, my ears!

Four

The Story of
"The Fertilised Ovum"

Tell me about the fertilised ovum, and about boys too.

All right. Actually the story of the fertilised ovum includes boys, so why don't I begin with them?

This is what a boy looks like.

But he's got no clothes on!

I know – I can't show you the private parts of a boy's body if he's dressed, can I?

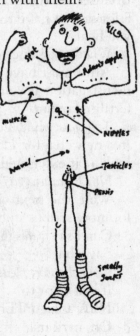

Here they are in close up:

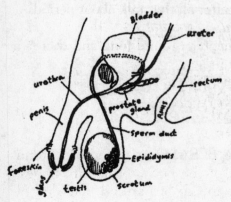

Another name for the "private parts" is the **genitals**. Unlike us girls, a boy's genitals are on the **outside**. Boys have a **penis** and **testicles**. The testicles hang in a bag of skin called the **scrotum**. The testicles are important because that's the place where special sex cells are made. These sex cells help to make a baby.

And a baby starts life as a . . .?

Fertilised ovum?

Very good! That's right.

And I was only guessing.

Well, it was a good guess. Let's go back to "cells" for a moment. Every human being is made up of cells. These are like tiny, microscopic building-bricks.

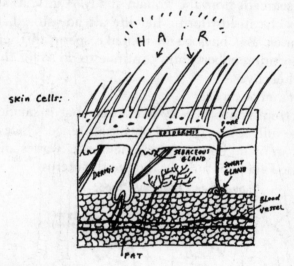

Skin Cells:

Millions and millions of them join together to form all the various parts of the body. Your skin, bones, lungs, heart, blood, and so on, are all made up of different cells.

New cells are continuously developing as old cells die away. Even though we are now made up of millions and millions of cells, it wasn't always like that. Believe it or not, we all started life when two cells joined together to form a new cell.

Where did these two cells come from?

One cell came from your mother and the other came from your father.

And how did these cells join?

Ah, we're back now to the fertilised ovum.

I told you earlier that there are **two ovaries** in a woman's body. These ovaries contain thousands of ova. Ova is plural for **ovum**, meaning "egg". These are the **sex cells** from the woman's body. A girl has all the eggs she needs during her life already stored in her ovaries. But boys begin to make sperm in their testicles during puberty and continue to do so for the rest of their lives.

What's an ovum like?

An ovum is a tiny, jelly-like speck that is smaller than the full stop at the end of this sentence. Once a month, an ovum moves out of one of the ovaries and down the Fallopian tube, leading to the uterus.

OVUM IN FALLOPIAN TUBE:

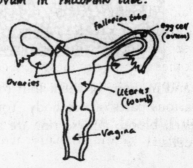

Now let's turn to the man's body again. His sex cells are made in the testicles. The male sex cells are called **sperm** and they are carried in a milky liquid called **semen**.

They too are jelly-like specks but they are much smaller than an ovum. Sperm have long tails which allow them to make a swimming movement.

Sperm (Enlarged Picture)

But if one cell is in the woman and the other is in the man, how do they join?

I'm just coming to that. The cells join when a man and a woman **make love**. Making love is also called **sexual intercourse**. When a man and a woman love each other very much, they show their love in many different ways. **Making love** is just one of these ways, but it's a very special one because it can make a baby. It starts when the man and the woman feel very warm and smoochie together, like when they're in bed. They lie close together and begin to kiss and cuddle. This has an effect on their bodies. The woman's vagina becomes **moist** and **stretchy** and the man's penis becomes **erect**. That means it becomes hard and stands out from his body. They are now ready to make love.

The man's erect penis fits snugly inside the woman's moist vagina. Because they are sexually excited, they move a lot together. This leads to **orgasm**.

Orgasm for the man is called **ejaculation**.

Orgasm for the woman is experienced **in the muscles of her vagina**. This is a very nice feeling for the woman and the man. At the moment of ejaculation semen comes out of the top of the man's penis. Semen is the milky liquid containing all the sperm.

How many?

Oh, millions and millions of them. I told you, they're tiny.

Anyway, the sperm come out of the top of the penis inside the woman's vagina. That's when they begin to swim – up further inside the woman's body, their little tails pushing them along as they search for an ovum.

Why are you laughing?

I'm imagining the ovum playing Hide-and-Seek with all the sperm inside the Fallopian tubes.

Well, that's more or less what happens. The sperm wriggle around looking for an ovum. If the sperm find one, they all mill around it until one of the sperm joins with it to make a new cell. Flip the book over to page 14 in *Boyfacts*. Peter has an illustration of this for the boys but you can look at it.

So there are millions of sperm and just one ovum?

Yes.

The ovum must feel very popular with all those sperm showing an interest in it!

I've never thought of it like that but I suppose you're right. The ovum is the centre of attention.

Does a baby start every time a man and a woman make love?

No. Sometimes the ovum is not in the right place for fertilisation to happen so the sperm can't find it to join together with it, or the man and woman might use some form of **contraception**. Contraception means preventing the sperm and ovum from joining together inside the womb. There are many means of contraception. People choose the kind that suits them.

Some people prefer to use methods which are **natural**. For example, a woman can calculate when an ovum is likely to be expelled from one of her ovaries. By making love at those times when the ovum isn't in the right place to meet the sperm, it's impossible for the two cells to join. The couple then avoid making love at those times when the ovum is likely to be fertilised.

Other methods are known as **artificial**. These include a contraceptive pill called a **combined pill** which stops ova from leaving the ovaries. If there's no ovum to be fertilised, a baby doesn't start. Sometimes people use **condoms.** A condom is like a little rubber bag that stretches over the erect penis and catches the sperm when it comes out.

Making babies, having sex and using contraception are private matters which mothers and fathers should think carefully about. Making babies is a big responsibility and so too is rearing a family.

I've one more question for you. What happens to all the other sperm that don't join with the ovum?

Oh, they all just die away because they aren't

needed any more. You see, once a sperm joins with the ovum, no other sperm can get in. It's like a **sealed unit**. Once this joining happens, a **new life** has started. A baby has begun. This is the moment of conception. The miracle of life.

And you've forgotten to tell me what a fertilised ovum is.

No, I haven't. You see, this new cell, made when the ovum is joined by the sperm, is now called the fertilised ovum.

New chapter, please.

Five
After the Birth

Now that you know about the fertilised ovum, I take it that you've no more questions.

Oh yes, I have. Loads of them!

For example?

Well, what happens to the baby while it's growing in the womb?

And how is a baby born?

And why are some babies girls and others are boys?

And how do you make twins?

And what happens when . . .

Hold on a minute! I'll be talking for *hours* if I have to answer all these questions. Hey, I've an idea. I'm going to make myself a cup of tea. In the meantime, here's what you'll do. I know Peter talked about all that in *Boyfacts*. Why don't we cheat and have a look at what's there, but for heaven's sake, don't get caught!

Flip the book upside down now and read from page 17 to page 21.

I'll be back by the time you're finished. Ready? Off you go now.

And good luck!

Ah, you're back.

Yeah. That was deadly. I loved the bit where the baby talks when it's being born.

Actually I like that part myself. I often think that that's what babies really would say if they could talk while being born. Tell me, have you any more questions?

Buckets of them!

What happens to the umbilical cord?

And why do some babies cry after being born?

When you've answered those, I'll ask you some more.

Perhaps it would be a good idea if I told you everything that happens to the baby after it has been born.

Let's go back to the moment of birth. Immediately after coming into the world, the baby must fill its lungs and start to breathe. The midwife or doctor must check that the baby's mouth and nose aren't blocked by fluid. Crying helps to clear the baby's breathing system. Then the baby is given to the proud parents to hold and cuddle for a few minutes. They've waited for nine long months to see their baby so it's a wonderful moment for them. Although it's the mother who gives birth, it's a good idea for the father to be around at this time. He can help and support the mother, and keep her company at this important moment in their lives. Unfortunately, sometimes the father isn't there when the baby is being born but most want to be present.

However, while the proud parents might be very happy, some babies definitely aren't. They just cry and cry and cry.

My Mum says I cried all the time.

And you can imagine why, of course. The womb is such a warm and cosy place, babies don't want to leave it. Inside the womb, the baby is as comfortable as could be, surrounded by liquid and darkness, with the sound of its mother's heartbeat for company. Then everything changes rather suddenly at the moment of birth. It must come as quite a shock to the baby. Having to leave this safe place and come out into the world is quite a change. That's why doctors and nurses try to make birth as quiet and gentle as they can.

Some mothers decide to have their baby at home so that things can be as normal as possible, but they still must have proper medical care and attention in case there's a problem.

I don't remember being born.

Nobody does, but it happened to all of us once upon a time. That was our first birthday.

And what happens to the umbilical cord?

The baby is still attached to the **placenta** by the umbilical cord, and the placenta is still attached to the womb inside the mother. So these must now be separated.

First the umbilical cord is clamped in two places and then cut between the clamps.

Then they do hurt the baby!

No, of course they don't. You see, there are no nerves in the umbilical cord so it doesn't hurt at all. It doesn't hurt you when your hair is cut, does it? It's the same with the umbilical cord. The little part left attached to the baby's navel is folded back and stuck down with a plaster. After a few days, this scab falls off and the navel heals.

And what happens to the placenta?

That's easy. The placenta also separates from the side of the womb and comes out of the mother's body through the birth canal. This is called the **afterbirth**. When this happens, the birth process is complete.

What else do they do to the baby?

Ah, back to the baby. Let me see now. The baby must be carefully checked to see that everything is working normally. It must also be weighed. This is important because, from now on, regular weight checks will tell whether it is growing up healthily. The baby must also be measured.

By now the nurse will have attached a bracelet to the baby's wrist telling its name and the date and time of birth. They do this to prevent any mix-up in the hospital. They don't want new parents to bring home the wrong baby, do they?

And of course the baby might want to be fed.

How is a new-born baby fed?

Generally, the mother **breast-feeds** it. When a woman is pregnant, her breasts begin to produce and to store milk. Then when the baby is born, she has a supply ready for when the baby wants it. The baby sucks the milk through the mother's nipples. A mother's milk is the best possible food for a baby because it's the food that nature itself provides. For the length of time that a mother suckles her baby, her breasts will continue to produce milk. A baby is weaned when the baby is taken off mother's milk and given other types of milk or more solid food instead.

Does the baby feel very cold when it's born?

Well, after the comfort of the womb, even a very warm room must seem cool to the baby. So newborn babies are wrapped up well in warm blankets. The baby's head must also be carefully covered as they can lose a lot of heat this way.

Babies can't do anything for themselves, can they?

Tiny babies depend totally on their parents for everything, but they can do some things. Babies can cry, cough, feed, sneeze and yawn. They can also see, hear and feel pain . . .

And babies have certain reflex actions such as sucking and gripping things with their tiny hands.

All newborn babies look the same, don't they?

No they don't. All newborn babies are different. You'll have to take a closer look next time you have a chance.

I already have and I still think they're all the same.

Have I answered all your questions?

No, not yet. Tell me about when things go wrong? You know, the problems and complications.

Then you'll have to turn the page.

Another new chapter, please.

Six

complications

What exactly do you want to know?

Why are some babies put in incubators? My Mother says I was in one for a week.

An **incubator** is like an enclosed glass cot in which some babies are placed immediately after being born.

You know that a baby in the womb needs **nine months** or **40 weeks** in which to grow to full-term. Then it's ready to be born.

But if a baby is born after only 28 weeks, it will still stand a good chance of survival if it gets proper medical care. By the way, babies who are born early, that is before the full nine months are up, are said to be **premature**.

Perhaps the baby might be very tiny and underweight when it's born, or the baby might have an infection or defect, so it's good for these babies to be placed in an incubator. That way they can receive the special care and attention that they need in order to survive. Many babies who are placed in incubators quickly catch up on babies who are full term.

What's it like for the baby inside the incubator?

Well, it's very warm and comfortable for the baby

because the incubator is kept at an ideal temperature. There's a nice soft mattress to lie on, and if anything goes wrong with the baby's breathing, an alarm sounds. The incubator is made of glass so that the mother and the hospital staff can see the baby at all times.

What does obstetrician mean?

An **obstetrician** is a doctor who specialises in pregnancy and childbirth.

And what's a forceps delivery?

The word **delivery** means birth. If a mother experiences difficulties with birth, the obstetrician may have to help her deliver her baby. Without this help, the consequences for the baby could be very serious.

FORCEPS DELIVERY:

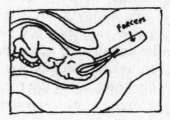

A **forceps** is a special implement that the obstetrician uses to fit snugly around the baby's head. Then the baby can be gently helped out through the vagina or birth canal.

But doesn't the forceps hurt the baby?

No, the baby isn't harmed in any way. Lots of babies need to be helped while they're being born. The forceps may leave a little mark for a while but it soon disappears without a trace.

What's a miscarriage?

You already know that a baby starts life as a fertilised ovum. At the very early stages, the fertilised egg is called an **embryo**, but eight weeks after conception it's called a **foetus**.

Well, a **miscarriage** is when the fertilised ovum fails to continue developing normally into a baby ready to be born.

Some babies never get beyond even the embryo stage or the foetus stage of life in the womb. Doctors have tried hard to find out why this happens but, most of the time, they just don't know the reason for it.

And then what happens to the fertilised ovum?

It comes out through the vagina as part of the menstrual discharge. Miscarriage usually happens quite early in pregnancy while the foetus is tiny. Sometimes it passes out with the period discharge without even being noticed, as the mother may not even have been aware that she was pregnant. But when the parents know about the pregnancy, the loss of a baby through a miscarriage can be very distressing for them.

What does abortion mean?

Abortion means the deliberate removal of the unborn baby from the uterus. Abortion is not the same as contraception. Contraception stops the ovum from ever meeting the sperm, so there won't be any fertilised ovum in the uterus. Abortion happens after the ovum has been fertilised.

Can a baby be born dead?

Unfortunately, yes. This is called **stillbirth** and it

happens if a mother gives birth to a baby who is dead. Parents are heartbroken when their baby is stillborn but nowadays medical care is so good that it doesn't happen as often as it used to in the past.

What's a Down syndrome baby?

Ah, we'll have to go back to Mathematics to answer that. Do you remember what you read about **chromosomes** in *Boyfacts*?

There are 23 chromosomes in the ovum from the mother and there are 23 chromosomes in the sperm from the father.

So in the fertilised ovum, the 23 from the ovum match with the 23 from the sperm. That makes 23 matched pairs, 46 chromosomes in all. Exact copies of these 23 matched pairs are passed to every cell in the baby's body, and these copies stay with it for the whole of the baby's life right through to old age.

Wow!

Well, sometimes an extra chromosome appears, and this causes all kinds of disorders in the baby. This extra chromosome can come from either the father or the mother. So instead of a normal matched pair of a certain type, the third chromosome appears and spoils everything because that extra chromosome now makes it 47 chromosomes in total. This extra chromosome interferes with the pairing process and has a great effect on the physical and mental development of the baby. That's what causes Down syndrome.

Defective genes are the cause of many of the other mental and physical disabilities that affect babies while they are developing in the womb. Sometimes complications arise immediately before or during birth, and these too can affect the baby.

Now, what else do you want to know?

Why do children look like their parents in certain ways?

Do you mean colour of eyes, hair, and so on?

Yeah, things like that.

We'll have to stay with chromosomes to answer this as well. Each chromosome contains thousands of **genes**. Genes are extremely complicated chemicals containing all the **instructions** that make up a person. The instructions about colour of hair and eyes are carried in just one gene each from the mother and the father. If the instructions in the genes are different, then the stronger gene becomes **dominant**. Your hair and eyes will then be decided by this stronger gene. The weaker gene is called a **recessive** gene. Dominant genes can come from either the mother or the father. With regard to hair genes, a dark-coloured hair gene is dominant over all other hair colours.

Isn't it fascinating to see what genes you've inherited from your mother's side of the family or from your father's side?

By the way, all the instructions about the changes that happen to people as they grow from the baby-stage right through to full adulthood are contained in these genes.

Will you tell me now about all the changes that happen to girls when they start to develop?

Ah, you want to know about **puberty**. There's so much to tell you that we'll need a new chapter. Why don't you go and have a good look at yourself in the mirror now before you read on. That way you can imagine how much changing you're going to do.

(NEW CHAPTER, PLEASE.)

It looks like we're going to need lots more space.

WARNING

The next chapter is for

GIRLS

o n l y

BOYS KEEP OUT
GO **NO** FURTHER

NO TRESPASSERS ALLOWED

DEFINITELY
NO BOYS

PRIVATE

Seven
Puberty for girls

In this chapter, I'm going to tell you all about **puberty**. That is the special time in a person's life when they change from being a **child** to being an **adult**. Yes, this happens to boys as well, but normally they're a bit later starting. We girls begin to develop first.

That's not surprising, is it? Girls are quicker at everything.

Oops! I hope nobody heard you say that. Dads wouldn't like it.

But Dads aren't boys.

Once upon a time they were. Then along came puberty and changed them into **men**.

So puberty's an important time?

Yes, very important. You see, these changes are not just **physical** (to do with the body). There are also **emotional** changes (to do with feelings), and **social** changes (to do with how we get on with other people).

Can you see these changes happening?

Not really, because puberty lasts many years. It may begin as early as nine or ten, and continue until you're around sixteen.

You may think that people grow at the same rate all the time, but they don't. There are two special times during our lives when we grow at a faster rate than normal. These stages are called **growth-spurts**. The first growth-spurt happened when you were a baby. Puberty is the second time when a growth-spurt occurs.

It can begin very quickly and you'll be surprised at how fast you'll grow in a short space of time. So too will your parents.

What makes puberty start in the first place?

I'll have to use some big words in this answer so listen very carefully to what I'm going to tell you.

Surprise! Surprise!

It all starts in the brain. There's a tiny part of your brain called the **hypothalamus**. Say HY-PO-THAL-A-MUS.

Hy-po-thal-a-mus.

Very good. Your hypothalamus sends **hormones** to . . .

What are hormones?

Hormones are chemical substances which are produced in the **endocrine glands**. And before you ask me what they are, here's an illustration to show you where the glands involved in growth are.

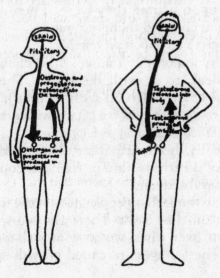

Now, where did I stop? Oh, yes, hormones. Your hypothalamus sends hormones to the **pituitary gland** in your brain. Then the pituitary gland starts to release other hormones which trigger off changes in the ovaries. They make ova develop and ripen.

Is it the same for boys?

Yes, the hypothalamus sends hormones in the same way to the pituitary gland in the boy's brain.

If he's got one . . .

. . . which in turn trigger off changes in the testicles. The testicles then start producing sperm. Both the ovaries and the testicles now begin to produce high levels of their own hormones. These hormones are now called the **sex hormones.**

What other changes happen to boys?

Well, apart from the biggest change, which is making sperm, there are many other more noticeable changes. For instance, he will start to grow much taller, his shoulders and chest will become broader, his face will change and his voice will break . . .

Then they won't be able to sing high notes anymore, will they?

And of course, hair will begin to grow on his face, chest, legs and pubic area.

Is that all?

Did I mention muscles? Boys become more muscular as they develop into men.

What happens to all the sperm that they make?

They are squeezed into the **epididymis**. This is like a coiled string that's attached to the testicle. They are stored here until they come out through the penis.

How does . . . ?

41

I'm just coming to that. When the epididymis is full, the sperm travel along sperm ducts towards the penis. Then they mix with a fluid called semen. When the penis goes hard, normally during the night when the boy is asleep, the semen spurts out of the top of the penis onto his tummy. This is called a **nocturnal emission** but it's more commonly known as a **"wet dream"**. If boys aren't expecting this to happen, it can be worrying for them but it's absolutely normal. In a fully-grown healthy man, the testicles produce several million sperm every day.

Did you say several million every day?

Yes.

Who counts them?

I'm not sure, but it has been done. Sperm are so tiny that several million take up no space at all.

You mentioned sex hormones a while ago. What do they do?

They help the ovaries and the testicles to continue maturing. And they also bring about all the other changes which occur during puberty.

In girls, the sex hormones are called **oestrogen** and **progesterone**, and in boys, the sex hormone is called **testosterone**.

That's an awful lot of hormones.

Yes, but you've an awful lot of growing to do, and without these hormones, this growth would not happen.

Sometimes I feel I don't want to grow up. I like being the way I am now.

I know what you mean. I sometimes felt the same way when I was your age, but growing up isn't so bad when you know what to expect. That's why I'm glad you're asking me all these questions.

Will you tell me more about changing?

♦ The first big change will probably be the **growth-spurt** I was telling you about a few moments ago. You'll know this because your clothes will get tight on you and your shoes will hurt.

♦ You'll get **taller**. In fact, you may even be taller than most of the boys in your class in school but they'll catch up on you in a year or two.

♦ You'll become **stronger** as your muscles develop.

♦ Your **breasts** will begin to develop. They may be very tender at first, and they may not grow evenly. This is quite normal. Your breasts will continue to grow for some years to come yet, so don't worry if they develop slowly or if they seem to be different for a while.

♦ Your **hips** will widen and become rounder.

♦ **Pubic hair** (the hair which grows in the genital area) will begin to appear and hair will also grow in your armpits.

♦ Your **face** will alter.

What? I thought that only happened to boys.

And to girls. Your forehead, nose and jaw will all grow, and this will change your face. But don't worry – you'll be more beautiful.

♦ Your **uterus** will increase in size, and so too will your vagina, but these changes won't bother you at all.

And there's the biggest change of all – **menstruation**.

Did you know that the special name given to a girl's first period is **menarche** (men-are-key)? This marks the start of puberty for a girl.

I've already told you a lot about your periods, so there's no need for me to explain it all again, but there's something very important for you to know.

When a girl begins her periods, it's a sign that she's old enough to have a baby, because it means that ova are ripening and travelling down through the Fallopian tubes.

And when a boy begins to produce sperm, it's a sign that he's old enough to help make a baby.

So young people have to be very **careful** and **responsible** about their behaviour when they're together, especially when they're in love. It's not a good idea for young people to make babies when they're not able to give them proper care and attention. But it *is* a good idea for people to say "NO" to sex until they are adult enough to take full responsibility for what they're doing.

Babies need their parents to be **mature and adult in every way**, and it takes years and years for all that maturing to take place.

Wow! Just think about it. All those changes start in our bodies all because of little things called hormones. And I once thought that growing-up was no sweat.

Ah, that reminds me. I never mentioned the **sweat glands**, did I?

No, you didn't. Are they important?

Well, your sweat glands will start to **work overtime** so it's vital to keep yourself **clean** from now on. Take regular baths and showers, and don't forget to brush your teeth often. Your hair may become greasy quite quickly, so wash it frequently with a good quality shampoo.

Do you bite your nails?
Of course I don't.
Then show me. Hmm! They're very short.
I gave up biting them an hour ago.
Did you now? Good for you.

That's at least ONE change you didn't need any hormones for.
Is that it?
Yes, I think so. Why?

NEW CHAPTER, PLEASE.

Shh! Not so loud.

Eight

More Facts about the Human Body

Did you know:

– that the biggest cell in the human body is the female ovum?

But of course.

– that the smallest cell is the male sperm?

– that a single male ejaculation may contain as many as 3,000,000 sperm, each of which can fertilise an ovum?

– that muscles make up about 35%-40% of the body's total weight?

Wow! No kidding?

Can you name some other important body parts that have nothing to do with sex and making babies?

Sure, I can. Bones! Muscles! Heart! Lungs! Tummy! Skin!

Very good.

Actually, these are the major systems in the human body.

Skeleton, skin and hair, heart and blood, digestion, respiration, muscles, nerves and brain.

I'm going to tell you a little about each.

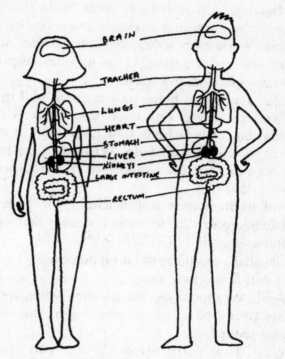

BRAIN

TRACHEA

LUNGS

HEART

STOMACH

LIVER

KIDNEYS

LARGE INTESTINE

RECTUM

Take your **skeleton** for instance.

It's your bones that give your body its shape. Otherwise it would be floppy and end up in a heap on the floor, just like a jellyfish. Inside most human bones, there are hollow cavities which are filled with **bone marrow**. This is important for making new blood cells. In total, the adult human skeleton has around 206 bones.

When you fracture a bone, the cells immediately begin to join together again to repair the break. The bone must be kept still for this to happen. That's why they put it in plaster-of-Paris.

Muscles help your body parts to do their work properly by providing strength and mobility. Some muscles work even when we're not conscious, e.g. breathing and digesting. Our muscles respond to messages sent from the brain.

Your **diaphragm** helps your lungs to pull in clean air and to pump out used air. This is called **ventilation**, or breathing. Our lungs take in **oxygen** and expel **carbon dioxide**. Without a continuous supply of oxygen, we would lose consciousness and die.

And what about your stomach?

I know. Mine rumbles when it's empty and when it's full it does this: BUH-URRRR-RPP!

Oh, that's rude. You did it on purpose.

Didn't! It just came out.

Well, you should say "Excuse me!" when you make a rude noise. Now, where was I? Oh, yes, we were talking about food.

Well, that's **digestion**. When you chew, or masticate, the food in your mouth is mixed with **saliva**. Saliva helps us to swallow our food. It then goes into the stomach which can stretch to hold more food. That's why you sometimes feel like bursting after you eat a big meal – your stomach is holding a lot of food.

Then it goes through the intestines where it is digested.

Finally, the waste material is stored in the rectum until it is expelled through the anus. So you see, a lot happens to your food after you swallow it.

Is it true that skin is waterproof?

Yes, it is. Actually, skin is like a fabric that covers and protects our bodies.

Why is a newborn baby's skin so wrinkled?

Because while in the womb its floating in **amniotic fluid,** which is a liquid, for months. I'm sure your skin is wrinkled after you have a warm bath. It's the same with a baby's skin.

Your skin is also part of your body's **immune system**. That means it's part of your body's natural defences against attack by **germs** or **infection**. Skin is quite tough and can repair itself when damaged. Sometimes when the cut is too big, stitches are needed to hold the skin together when it's healing. The only things that naturally penetrate your skin are hair and sweat pores. Your skin, especially your hands, needs regular washing to help it guard against infection.

How does an infection pass from one person to another?

Bacteria are very small organisms made up of single cells. They can only be seen under a microscope. Most bacteria live in the soil, in water or in decaying matter. Bacteria are also present all over the surface of your skin.

Ugh!

Don't worry. Washing and bathing reduce the chances of infection. Anyway, there are different kinds of bacteria. Some bacteria are good, others are harmless, but certain bacteria are deadly. They cause diseases such as typhoid, cholera and tuberculosis. Because they live in the soil or in water, it's possible for humans to "catch" them by eating or drinking contaminated foods or liquids. They can also be "caught" if we breathe in air which has already been breathed, sneezed or coughed out by an infected person. It's possible to be infected by touching an infected person also, or if the bacteria attack through an open wound or sore.

Wow, that's scary.

No, not really. The body has many defences. I've already told you one of them.

I know. Skin. It's part of the Immune System.

That's right, and, of course, the **white cells** in blood are a great defence tool. The white cells cluster around any harmful bacteria and eventually kill it. Blood also manufactures chemicals called **antitoxins** which kill the poisonous effects of the bacteria. Once we recover from an infection, our blood is much stronger and is better able to fight that infection if it attacks again. This process helps us to acquire **immunity**.

Can doctors help us to acquire immunity?

They certainly can. Sometimes they deliberately give people a mild dose of an infection so that their blood will form **antibodies** as protection from any further attack.

That's clever.

That's called **immunisation**.

Like the MMR?

What does that stand for?

Mumps, Measles, Rubella.

Correct. By giving you a mild dose of MMR, doctors make sure that your body's immune system will be able to fight these infections if they ever attack you.

What's a virus?

Gosh, this is turning into a discussion on Biology. A **virus** is an organism much smaller than a bacteria. Because it's so small, it can pass through filters that will keep out bacteria. Viruses only live in plants and animals that are themselves alive. They spread in the same way as bacteria. When conditions are right, they can multiply rapidly and cause great harm. Diseases such as polio and smallpox are caused by a virus. So too are influenza – the flu – and the common cold.

And AIDS?

Yes, AIDS is caused by a virus. It's called the HIV. The V stands for Virus. If a person is carrying the virus, they are said to be HIV Positive. HIV carriers can pass on the virus to another person. That's why people are being told to practice safe sex, so that they won't be infected with the AIDS virus or any other kind of sexual disease.

What are STDs?

Ah, STD stands for Sexually Transmitted Diseases. These diseases are passed from one person to another mostly by close contact during sexual activity. The virus can easily pass from one person's body to another. That's way people are warned to be very careful about their sexual behaviour.

When I had the flu last year, the doctor gave me antibiotics.

I bet you didn't know that **antibiotics** are chemicals actually made from bacteria. They help the body to recover from many illnesses by killing the bacteria without harming the body. However, while there is no cure yet for the AIDS virus, some medications are now used to slow the progression of HIV-related diseases.

I've heard enough about bacteria and viruses. Tell me something different.

Did you know that each square inch of skin has:

- 19,000,000 cells?
- about 60 hairs?
- about 19 feet of blood vessels?
- over 600 sweat glands?
- nearly 100 oil glands?

Of course I knew all that. Do you think I have no brain?

Now that you've mentioned it, I should also tell you a little about your brain. First, I'm glad you know you have one.

Very funny!

The brain is the **control centre** of the body. Messages travel to all parts of your body along the **spinal cord** and **nerves**. The brain is much more complex than any computer and scientists are still mystified as to how it works.

Did you know that the brain is made up of about 30,000,000,000 cells? Impressive, don't you think?

Even boys' brains? They couldn't be.

I bet you couldn't read "30,000,000,000" out loud.

Can so.

Say it then.

Thirty . . . em . . . thirty . . . eh!

Thirty thousand million.

Well, it is a big number . . .

Excuses, excuses!

Time for a new chapter!

Nine
Keeping Safe

You know how important it is to keep your body healthy but it's also very important to keep your body safe. There are times when you must be extra careful, like when you're crossing the road or cycling your bike. Of course rules exist to help you, but as you get older, you learn to use your judgement as well as your common sense.

Take **touching**, for instance.

Common sense tells us that certain types of touches are not acceptable, like hitting, kicking and punching, for example, but other touches are good, like a hug from your parents when you feel lonely or sad, or a goodnight kiss when you're going to bed. Sometimes when you are ill, or if you have to go for a check-up, a doctor or nurse might have to examine you. They may have to touch you, perhaps even on the private parts. These touches also are okay, because there is a good reason for them. If you have a rash or a sore on the private parts of your body, you may have to show them to your parents first, so that they can decide what attention you need.

Apart from proper reasons for touching or examining your body, nobody has the right to touch you. If anyone does touch you in a way that you know is wrong, then you must tell, no matter what this other person says.

How would I know if touches were okay?

Perhaps this rule will be helpful for you:

If any touch or suggestion makes you feel bad, or embarrassed, or ashamed, or unsafe, you must tell someone about it. That includes any touching of the private parts of the body by another person who has no proper reason or permission to do it.

That's when you tell.

What if I'm not sure?

Then tell someone about it anyway.

What if nobody listens to me?

Then keep telling until they do. They'll soon see you're serious, and will try to help you.

What can I do now to help keep myself safe?

The obvious rules are:

◆ Make sure your parents know where you are at all times and come home at agreed times

◆ Talk to your mother and father about answering the phone.

◆ Don't ever tell your name to people you don't know

◆ Play in places where there are plenty of people around.

◆ Say "no" to suggestions that are wrong, risky, foolish or dangerous

◆ If you know something is wrong, then don't do it and if you're asked to do something wrong, tell immediately.

◆ If your have your own mobile phone, don't talk to anyone you don't know. Hang up immediately and tell your parents. If anyone sends you a rude or bullying text message, anonymously, show it to your parents immediately. Of course you should never pass on a hurtful message either. It's fun having your own phone but you must be responsible as well.

I know all those rules already. What else can I do?

You could also discuss some other situations with your parents. For example, what would you do:

◆ If you were separated from your parents in a strange place?

◆ If someone knocked at the door when you were home alone?

◆ If someone wanted to steal your money on the way home from school?

◆ If you were asked to do something you didn't want to do, e.g. smoke, steal, damage property, lie touch somebody else's private parts, take drugs etc?

◆ If you were asked to go somewhere that your parents didn't approve of?

◆ If you were asked not to tell about something which you knew was wrong?

◆ If someone you didn't know chased you?

◆ If you were being bullied?

◆ If you were in trouble, and were afraid to tell at home?

◆ If somebody was hitting you, hurting you or harming you in any way and you were afraid of them?

So you see, there's a lot to think about when it comes to keeping yourself safe. Now that you're getting older and more independent, you won't need to have your mother and father around you all the time. So it's important for you to know in advance what to do in certain situations.

Make your plans now.

Then, no matter what happens, you'll know the right thing to do.

But the golden rule is always to TELL! TELL! TELL!

Ten

Attraction

Do you watch much television?

No, hardly ever.

What do you think of the advertisements?

Some are real cool but others are awful, especially the washing powder ones. I hate those.

I know what you mean, but advertisements try to show us all kinds of things looking their best. Otherwise we wouldn't want to buy them, would we? There's nothing attractive about soap powders or food mixers or dog food or razor blades or . . .

Dogs find dog food attractive.

Very funny. You know what I mean. Advertisers work very hard to make us go out and buy their goods. That's what they're paid for. But of course we can choose to buy what we like, or we can keep our money.

I bet advertisers don't like that, do they?

No, I suppose not.

Did you ever notice that advertisements are very limited in what they can do? They can only show us appearances, images and pictures to make their product look good, and they hope that this will make us go out and spend our money.

Sometimes they use models (mostly young women) to make the product look more glamorous, but you don't get the model when you buy a packet of crisps or a soft drink, do you? And sometimes, the products aren't as good as they look on television. That's because the advertisements can only show us appearances.

But the models are real, aren't they?

Of course the models and actors are real people, but they are not showing us real life. We can't tell from watching an advertisement whether the actor or model is kind, considerate, cheerful, dull, boring, and so on. All we can see is what the person looks like: we can't tell what kind of person she or he is.

It's important to know more about people than just how they look, isn't it?

Yes, it is. That's why we should learn to appreciate all the other qualities and skills that people have and not just be attracted by looks alone.

My goldfish is gorgeous. His mouth always makes an O-shape.

Ah, yes. Pets. They're very attractive. People like to stroke them and hold them in their arms. Pets are very good company.

Babies are cute too. They're so warm and cuddly.

Yes, it's interesting that most people find babies and pets attractive. And people find each other attractive also.

Men are attracted to women and women are attracted to men. A person who is attracted to the opposite sex is called a **heterosexual**.

Could a person be attracted to a member of their own sex?

Yes. Some men find they are more sexually attracted to other men rather than to women and some women find they are more sexually attracted to other women rather than to men. These people are called **homosexuals** or gays. Homosexual women are also known as lesbians.

It's impossible to tell by looking at another person whether they are heterosexual or homosexual. Appearances can give a false impression, and if we judge a person by looks alone, we won't ever know what that person is really like.

Some boys call others names.

Yes, this can happen. For instance, a boy might be called a "homosexual" or some other word just because he is friendly with another boy; or a girl might be called a "lesbian" or some other word because she is friendly with another girl. This is very wrong.

Calling others names can spoil friendships and cause great upset and hurt, so no name-calling, please.

It's good to make new friends, isn't it?

Of course it is. That's part of growing up. You'll change from one school to another, and from one class to another. You'll join different clubs, and perhaps take up new interests and sports. All this will help you to meet different people and make new friends. When you make a new friend, it doesn't mean that you lose all your old ones. It's just that your circle of friends gets bigger. Of course, it's nice to have a special friend in whom you can confide, but it's also nice to have lots of friends, and the best way of keeping friends is to be a friend.

Some friends are special.

Perhaps, later on when you're older, you'll fall in love and want to be with someone special a lot of the time.

Then you'll want to take better care with your appearance. You'll keep yourself cleaner, washing your hair regularly and spraying yourself with deodorant.

I do all that already.

Then when you go out on a date or you just want to hang out together, you'll feel good and look good. Here's something for you to think about. It may only take a while to get ready to go out in one way, but in another way, it takes years and years.

What do you mean?

I'm talking about maturing. It takes time for people to grow up enough to be able to take responsibility for themselves when they're away from home for a while. And when young people begin dating, their parents have to be sure that they're safe, wherever they are. So it's wise to talk to your parents about what's allowed before you begin having a special relationship. Girls especially come under pressure to do things that can lead to sex, so talking to your parents first is a very good idea. Don't be afraid to say "no" to things that you're not happy with. Kissing can be nice, but it can also lead to trouble. I know Peter has said that to the boys as well. Young people have to be careful about their behaviour.

Eleven

Families

You know that people come in all shapes and sizes.

Well, it's the same with families. Some families are larger, with four or more children; others are smaller, having just one or two. Regardless of how many children there are in the family, they have certain needs that must be provided for. For example, all children need:

- loving care and attention
- food, clothing and warmth
- to be safe
- to be kept clean
- healthcare
- sleep.

As well as these needs, which are physical, children have other needs which have to do with learning.

Not school again?

No, not school-learning. I'm talking about the other kinds of learning that people must do. For example, learning about:

- correct behaviour
- the difference between right and wrong
- how to get on with others
- good personal habits and skills.

This kind of learning goes on all the time. But you mentioned school just now. Children have a right to a good education, which will help them to prepare for a happy and fulfilled adult life.

What's the greatest need?

That's easy. All people, small or big, need **love**.

But parents are different, aren't they?

All people are different. We all have good points and bad points, strengths and weaknesses, talents and ability. Some people are very good at bringing up their children, others find it more difficult. It's hard to be a good parent all the time, but it's important to try.

That's why I told you earlier that people should

wait until they are mature and grown-up in every way before they have children of their own. There is a huge difference between

(a) being able to **make a baby**; and

(b) being able to **be a parent**.

Sometimes parents have to face serious problems in their lives and it's not possible for the mother and the father to continue being together. There are many different reasons for this. For example, as people grow older, they change in many ways. And just as two people can fall in love, they can also fall out of love.

Parents today have to deal with many pressures and problems and parents themselves can make all kinds of mistakes. A problem may begin with just one parent, but it ends up affecting both because they share a relationship. Or they both can contribute to the problem.

When parents have to face serious problems, it's very difficult for children not to be affected by what's happening. Children don't like to see their parents arguing, but fortunately most arguments are not serious and they're over quickly.

After all, it's very difficult to be good-humoured all the time. Obviously someone in the house is bound to fly off the handle at times. I'm sure even you are cranky every now and then.

But what do parents do if they have a very serious problem?

Well, parents may go to see a counsellor who will help them, or they may decide to separate while they try to solve their problem. Then again, one parent may choose to bring up a child (or children) alone. These parents are called lone or single parents. That's why some families may have one parent instead of two.

There are families where the mother or father has died. While some families lose a parent this way, there are others which gain extra people. Sometimes families have grandfathers and grandmothers living with them, or uncles and aunts, or even more distant relatives.

Some parents wish to adopt or foster a child, or perhaps more than one, and make them part of their very own family.

And don't forget that sometimes a couple choose not to have a family, or maybe they can't have children of their own because of some private difficulty or problem.

Now you know why I said at the beginning – that families come in all shapes as well as sizes – but no matter what shape or size a family is, all children need someone to love them and care for them.

Grown-ups need love too. In fact, love is what keeps families together and, if love is missing, it's very hard for families to stay together. It's love that helps us to grow into good adults and to become good parents when it's our turn to have children.

A Few Final Words

Well, I've told you nearly all you need to know so I'm going to take a rest now. I'm tired from all the thinking and talking you've made me do. Just remember that all the information I've given you is no good unless you can use it to help you make good choices and decisions as you get older.

Aw, don't go yet, Cathy. I'm enjoying our chat. Anyway, I've another question for you.

I doubt that I'll be able to answer it. I've used up all my answers.

What can I do if I forget some of the things you've told me?

Well, you just come straight back to me and we'll talk again. Now, why don't you take a break too and find something else to do? Surely you could polish some furniture or tidy your room or clean out the attic?

No, that's not what I have in mind.

Well, what is it then?

Could I . . . em . . .

What?

Eh . . .

You mean . . .?

Yeah!

Oh, all right then. Flip the book over and start again. I'm sure Peter and the boys won't really mind. I have to admit that I enjoyed reading *Boyfacts* myself so I'm sure you will too.

Happy reading.

It's OK to flip over now.

"Cheerful, matter of fact information and full of common sense, useful for parents as well as girls and boys."

Fionnuala Kilfeather
National Parents Council Primary

"The author, a teacher with wide experience of sex instruction, has done an excellent job in bringing plenty of useful information to an age group that often has difficulty in understanding it".

Irish Farmer's Journal

"This book would be ideal reading for girls and boys approaching the age of puberty, and would provide useful resource for teachers or parents in the provision of sex education for children".

Education Today

"A simple, practical and amusing book for any teacher or parent to use, making an awkward subject a lot easier to address".

Primary Times

Boyfacts

By Peter Bird

Boyfacts

By Peter Bird

Everything you ever wanted to know about a lot of stuff

Edited by Aidan Herron

POOLBEG

This edition 2006

Published 1995
by Poolbeg Press Ltd
123 Grange Hill, Baldoyle
Dublin 13, Ireland
E-mail: poolbeg@poolbeg.com

© Aidan Herron 1995

The moral right of the author has been asserted.

Typesetting, layout, design © Poolbeg Press Ltd.

3 5 7 9 10 8 6 4

A catalogue record for this book is available from the British Library.

ISBN 1-85371-504-2
ISBN 978 1 85371 504 4 (From January 2007)

Illustrations by Adrienne Geoghegan
Cover design and setting by Poolbeg Press Ltd.
Printing by Litografia Roses, Spain

www.poolbeg.com

To Brian

contents

Hello. This side of the book is for boys and it's full of facts. That's why it's called *Boyfacts*.

Message for Girls
Flip the book over because you're at the wrong end.
The other side of the book is for you.
(End of message for girls).

Boyfacts is all about the changes that take place in human beings as they develop from the baby stage to the grown-up stage. Peter will answer a lot of your questions about sex and growing-up, and he has also put in some extra chapters for good measure.

When you've read *Boyfacts* (and *Girlfacts* – but don't get caught reading their side), you'll probably know more about babies and growing-up and puberty than your parents do, so you should be prepared to explain things to them.

Perhaps you could also give them a loan of this book. After all, somebody has to tell parents about the *facts of life*, and who better than you, their son?

I hope you enjoy reading *Boyfacts*.

The Editor.

Psst! Girls, I know you're reading this. Don't get caught.

One
Let's Introduce Ourselves

Hi. I'm Peter Bird. I'm very pleased to meet you. This book is all about sex and growing up. It's full of information about things that you need to know, and, of course, you can ask me a question any time you like. When you ask a question, *you can talk to me in this kind of type.* Okay?

But before I say any more, we need to do a sex check. This part of the book is for boys.

So if you look like this . . .

. . . it's okay to read on.

BOY

But if you look like this . . .
. . . you've made a big mistake.
Flip the book over *immediately*.

GIRL

Okay. I think we're on our own now.

It's tough being a boy when there are so many nosey girls around, always looking over our shoulders, prying into our affairs, making trouble for us.

Actually, girls make up about 52% of the human race. I bet you didn't know that.

So what? They're always making out to be better than us. Sometimes it's impossible to get away from them for any length of time. Why can't they just leave us men alone?

You mean especially now when you want to talk about growing up and sex. Why are you blushing?

Well, "sex" is a bad word, isn't it? At least that's what all the lads say.

Of course sex isn't a bad word. But some people think it is and they're wrong. Maybe I'd better tell you about sex and growing up. How much do you know already?

I know it all.

Hmm! we'll see. Are there any girls around?

No.

Parents?

No.

The dog?

No.

Good! Okay, it's safe to read on.

Two
The Blue Treatment

Do you remember when nearly everything you had was blue?

Blue? What do you mean?

I'm talking about the time when you were just born. The chances are that you:

- were wrapped in a blue blanket
- were given lots of blue cuddly toys
- wore a blue babygrow
- used a blue dribbler
- sucked a blue soother.

And of course your room was painted blue. With blue curtains to match. And what about blue teddies? Blue carpet? Blue borders? Enough blue to make you blue in the face.

Why all this blue? Well, I don't really know the answer to that but it is one way of making it known very clearly that you were a boy and not a girl. Of course, there is another way of finding out whether you are a boy or a girl, and we don't need any colour to tell us, do we? Yep! You're right. Just take off your clothes. You're blushing again.

No, I'm not.

When babies are born, you can tell the difference between boys and girls by looking at their **genitals**. That's the name given to the **private parts** of a person's body.

So tell me something I don't know.

Okay. Turn the page.

Did you know that a mosquito has 47 teeth?

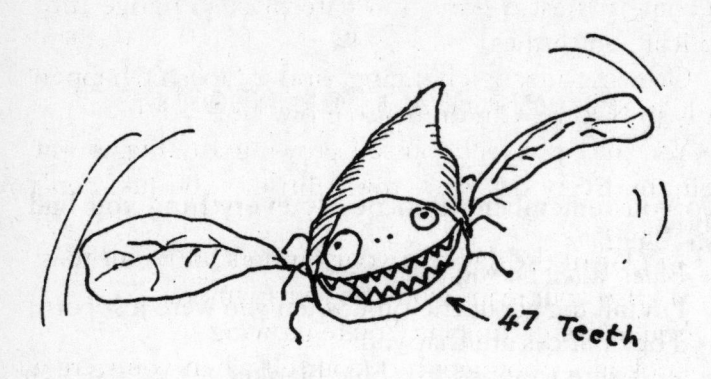

47 Teeth

Ha, ha! You didn't expect that, did you?

Right. It's time to stop fooling around. Let's get down to some serious talking. Take growing, for instance.

Have you ever thought that growing up is a marvellous time in everybody's life? People change from being tiny babies into fully-grown adults over a period of many years.

I'll bet girls take longer.

Actually, they don't. Everyone grows at their own rate.

I was only kidding.

As you grow up, you'll find out all sorts of things. Some of these things you'll learn at school, or at home, or from friends, or from television or even the internet. But learning maths, science, history and all the other subjects in school is not enough. You have to learn about growing too.

Look at all the growing that happens in Nature.

Tiny seeds become huge trees. Little cubs grow up to become majestic lions and caterpillars change into delicate butterflies.

Growing means changing, and it doesn't happen only in Nature. Children also grow.

You may not feel yourself growing any bigger but you are. Every day you grow a little – you just don't notice.

- ◆ Until the day that your runners hurt your toes
- ◆ Or your jeans won't fit you anymore.

You're not getting fat. You're growing.

Look at a photograph of yourself when you were a baby. Do you see how much you've changed since then? That's growing for you. Once upon a time you were tiny, ugly and wrinkled. Now look at you. HANDSOME! BRILLIANT! MATURE! JUST WAITING TO BE DISCOVERED.

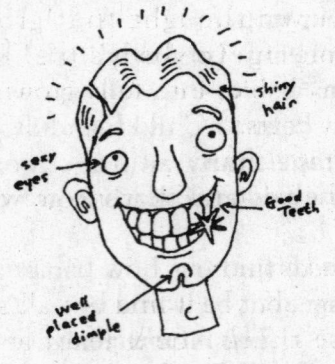

Your body has been working very hard from the time that you were a baby for all those changes to happen, but I'm not just talking about your body. Your mind has changed too and you can now do so much more.

You can walk, talk, think, read, write, cross the road, help around the house, and so on. You have developed hobbies and skills that you enjoy. You can join in all kinds of sports and games. Can you imagine yourself in a pair of baby shoes now, or in a buggy, or wearing a dribbler? Oh yes, you've changed a lot over the years, and you will continue to change for quite some years to come.

For example, you're not yet old enough to vote or to drive a car. Nor are you allowed to bungee jump or join the army, but you will some day, when you've grown enough.

Did you ever wonder why your parents came to be older than you, or how your grandparents came to be their age? It's because people are born at different times. Your grandparents started to grow a long time ago. Next it was your parents' turn to grow.

Now it's your turn.

For human beings (yes, even girls), growing means changing from

Baby to Child to Adult.

At that stage many adults choose to become parents themselves and that's how you came to be born.

If you want to find out how babies are made, turn to the next page, but be warned:

This information is
Top Secret!
Stop here
if you're not ready for
Major Discoveries

8

Three
The Big Step

So you've decided to take the big step.

I knew you would. Now take a deep breath and read on, but I have to tell you there's a lot of information in this chapter. To make sure that you've been paying attention, I'm going to ask you some tough questions at the end.

Let's begin by explaining some of the words that I'm going to use in this story.

You've heard the word "sex" before, but do you really know what it means?

"Sex" means the "difference between being male and female".

Because you're a boy, you belong to the male sex.

Girls belong to the female sex.

Now you see why the word "sex" is not a bad word.

Both males and females have private parts. The correct terms for the private parts of the body are the **genitals** or **sexual organs**. While these parts of the body may be used for removing urine (peeing), they also have another very important function.

Sound of trumpets please!

They're used for making babies.

Let's take a closer look at a girl's body first.

The **vulva** is the name given to the female genital area.

Girls have a special opening between their legs called the **vagina**, and their sexual organs are on the inside.

For boys, it's quite different. Our genitals are on the outside.

Boys have a **penis** and **testicles**.

The testicles are also known as "balls" because that's exactly what they look and feel like. The testicles are inside a pouch (or bag) of skin called the **scrotum.**

Each person's genital area is private and it's important to respect that privacy. It's also important to know about the genital area because without our sexual organs, it would be impossible for men and women to become fathers and mothers by making babies.

So how exactly are babies made?

Look at this illustration. Can you see what it is?

Yes, it's a cell.

Okay, it's not a great drawing but you get the general idea. Cells are Nature's Lego bricks, except that they're so small that they can't be seen without the help of a microscope. There's one in the middle of the circle on the next page.

11

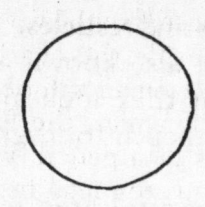

But you can't see it, can you? I told you, cells are small. Well, human beings are made of cells, millions and millions of them, but in the beginning, just two cells are needed to start a baby. One of these cells comes from the mother and the other cell comes from the father. When these two cells meet, they join together like two drops of water that become one. This new cell is the start of a new life.

Where do the cells meet?

Inside the mother's body.

How does this happen?

That's a very short question but the answer is a very long one. You'll have to listen carefully.

The cell from the mother is called an **ovum** (meaning egg). It's a little jelly-like speck that is smaller than a full-stop in a book. The ovum comes from a part of the mother's body called the ovary. There are two ovaries, one on either side of the uterus. Here's a picture to show you.

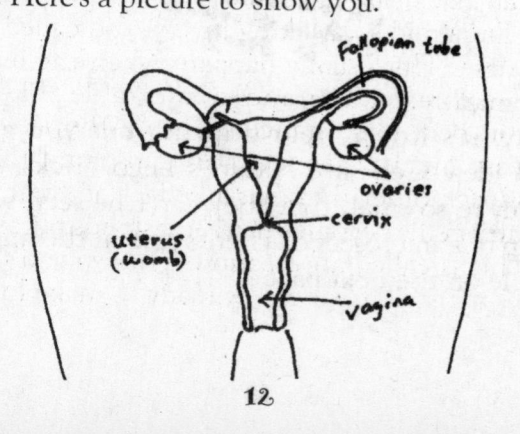

The ovaries are connected to the womb by the **Fallopian tubes**. Contained inside the ovaries are all the ova (plural of "ovum") a woman will need in her lifetime.

In a fully-grown woman, the Fallopian tubes are about the thickness of a pencil, while the inside of the tube is as thick as the lead inside the pencil. So you can see that the ovum manages to move along a very narrow tunnel indeed.

The cell from the father is called the **sperm**. Sperm are made in the testicles. They too are tiny jelly-like specks but they are much smaller than the ovum. Sperm have tails which allow them to move by a kind of swimming action. They are carried in a liquid called **semen**.

Both the ovum and sperm have to be in a liquid. Otherwise they would dry up and die.

When a baby has started, it grows in the **womb** (or **uterus**). This is the part of the mother's body specially reserved for the baby. Here it will grow and develop for nine months until it's ready to be born.

But you still haven't told me exactly how the cells from the mother and the father join together.

I'm just coming to that now. When a man and a woman want to make a baby, they have to **make love**.

Not all that kissing and mushy stuff?

Yes, I'm afraid so. Making love is also called **sexual intercourse**. This usually happens when the man and the woman feel warm and comfortable, like when they're in bed, for instance. Because they love each other very much, they feel very close and they hug and kiss each other. This has an effect on their bodies. The man's penis becomes hard and stands out from his body. This is called an **erection**. The woman's vagina becomes moist. They are now ready to make love.

13

The man slips his penis inside the woman's vagina and they begin to move together. Gradually this moving becomes more excited and when this excitement reaches a peak (or climax) they have an **orgasm**. This feels very nice for both of them.

Orgasm for the woman is when her **vaginal muscles contract**, while a man has an **ejaculation**. Sometimes they have an orgasm at the same time and sometimes they don't.

Ejaculation means that a milky liquid called **semen** comes out of the top of the man's penis. This is the liquid in which the sperm are carried. Millions and millions of sperm pass out of the man's body when he ejaculates.

Once inside the vagina, the sperm swim up through the womb, into the Fallopian tubes, in search of an ovum. When they meet an ovum, they all mill around until one of them joins together with it. At that very moment of joining, a new baby has started. A new life has begun. This is called **conception**.

The baby will now continue to grow in the womb until it is time for it to be born. When a woman is expecting a baby, she is said to be **pregnant**. She is now an expectant mother.

Sperm breaking into egg

Do people make a baby every time they make love?

No, not always. Some people experience difficulties when trying to make a baby. Others decide to use **contraception** to stop the ovum and the sperm meeting. This is called Family Planning. There are many methods of contraception. Some methods of contraception are simple, others more complicated. For example there are times when an ovum isn't in the right place for a sperm to meet it. When a couple make love at this time a baby usually doesn't start. This is called a **natural method** of contraception. Other women decide to take a contraceptive pill to stop an ovum leaving the ovary. This is called an **artificial method** of contraception. Of course, they may also decide to use a condom. This is like a little rubber bag which fits over an erect penis to catch the semen as it comes out. This is also an artificial method of contraception. There are many other methods but some are quite complicated. Contraception is a private matter for adults to decide.

How many babies could a woman have?

When you consider that pregnancy lasts for nine months, it's theoretically possible for a woman to have a baby nearly every year for many years. Of course this would be very tiring for her, and the parents would have huge families to mind and care for. It's a private matter for parents themselves to decide how many children they want to have.

Women have to take good care of themselves during pregnancy, don't they?

They certainly do. An expectant mother has to eat well, exercise and take plenty of rest, as she is carrying a new life within her body. She should try to

avoid alcohol and smoking, because the baby can be affected by them.

Do parents make love only when they want to make a baby?

No, not necessarily. Making love feels very nice for the mother and father. It's one of the ways that parents show that they love each other very much and that they are special to each other but, because it's such a special way of showing love, it's also private.

Does everyone start life this way?

Yes, all human being started life in this way, at the exact moment when two cells join.

Did I?

Yes, you too. A sperm from your father joined with an ovum from your mother to make you. And it was the same for your parents, and for your grandparents, and so on, back through your family. It was the same for everybody who has ever lived.

Now just to check that you've been paying attention, here are some questions for you:

1. How many teeth has a mosquito?
2. How thick are the Fallopian tubes?
3. What do you call the liquid that carries the sperm?
4. What is the other name for "making love?"

Very good. You have been paying attention.

Four

Life in the Uterus

On with the story.

After nine months the baby is ready to be born.

Hold on a minute. You never told me what it's like for the baby inside the uterus during the nine months.

Well, in that nine months, the baby grows from being smaller than the size of a full-stop (.) to "newborn-baby" size.

At the very beginning, the mother doesn't feel the baby inside her uterus but as it gets bigger, it starts to move and stretch and the mother will feel it.

Perhaps, if your mother or aunt is pregnant, maybe you could put your hand on her tummy to feel the baby move.

The fertilised ovum attaches itself to the lining of the womb and starts to develop. For the first ten weeks in the uterus, the developing baby is called an **embryo**. After that time, it is called a **foetus**. Even at this early stage, the sex of the baby is already fixed because the sperm from the father carries instructions to make the baby either a boy or a girl. So this new human being will grow inside the uterus as either a girl or a boy, depending on that instruction. The first eight or nine weeks of life in the uterus is a very important time. While it doesn't look very human in the beginning, little by little, the baby's head, arms, legs, feet, eyes, ears, nose and mouth take shape. By twelve weeks it does indeed resemble a real human being.

How can doctors tell if the baby is developing properly in the uterus?

One way is by carrying out an **ultrasound** examination.

What's that?

A machine sends sound waves right through the mother's body. These waves bounce off any surface inside her body and show up on a type of television screen in the form of a picture. It's possible to see the baby's arms, legs, and so on, and see how it's developing. They can also tell if the woman is expecting twins.

Can they tell if the baby has anything wrong with it?

Yes. Ultrasound examinations and blood tests may

show up certain problems with a baby, but in order to be fully sure doctors will have to examine some of the baby's cells. They do this by a test called **amniocentesis**. Doctors can obtain samples of the baby's cells from the fluid in the uterus. Of course they have to be very careful when they're doing this in order not to harm the baby. The sample is then tested in a laboratory.

Can they tell whether it's a boy or a girl?

Yes, an examination of the baby's cells will tell whether it's a girl or a boy, but many parents prefer not to be told. They like the surprise.

How does the baby in the uterus feed?

Good question. I can see that you're really wide awake. Human beings need food and oxygen to grow and live. But the baby in the uterus can't feed and breathe the same way that we do. It gets its food and oxygen from its mother's blood.

From its mother's blood? You're kidding.

No, I'm not.

But you make babies in the uterus sound like vampires.

Let me explain. There's a special tube called the **umbilical cord** which connects the baby to the mother. One end of the umbilical cord is attached to the **placenta**, which is attached to the lining of the uterus, and the other end is attached to the baby's tummy.

Where my belly-button is?

Exactly – your navel. All the baby's food is carried in the mother's blood through the placenta, along the **umbilical cord** and into the baby's body.

So how does the baby go to the toilet? There's no potty in the uterus, is there?

No, there isn't, but babies in the uterus need to get rid of waste from their bodies, just as we do from ours. Waste material from the baby's body travels back along the umbilical cord and through the placenta. In fact, the placenta does the work of the lungs, kidneys, intestines and glands.

The placenta also prevents some harmful substances from getting through to the baby. But mothers still have to be careful with smoking and taking alcohol or drugs when they're expecting a baby because some of the chemicals in these drugs can actually cross through the placenta and harm the baby.

The baby is very comfortable in the womb because it's floating around in a sort of bag (sometimes called a sac) filled with a liquid called **amniotic fluid**. This amniotic fluid helps to keep the baby warm and to save it from bumps.

The baby can bounce around quite freely in this fluid. It can kick, push and stretch inside its mother. Sometimes you can even see and feel its movements as it pushes against the uterus.

But as it grows, it has less and less room to move around because it begins to fill all the available space in the uterus. The same thing happens when a mother is expecting twins. Her uterus expands as the babies grow bigger. After some time, it becomes very noticeable that a woman is pregnant.

Babies in the uterus can hear sounds and voices as well as their mother's heartbeat. They spend some time sleeping and then wake up. Unborn babies are often very active. Some even suck their thumbs.

All during pregnancy, a mother has to take good care of her health by eating well and exercising regularly. Some mothers experience **morning sickness**

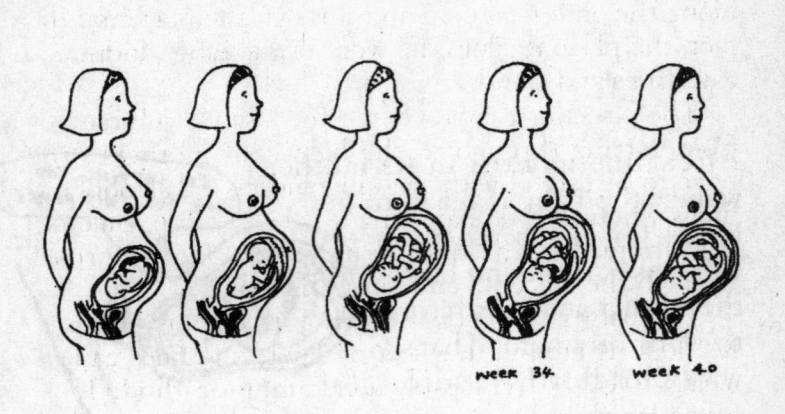

week 34   week 40

(vomiting) but this passes after a while. Mothers can also feel a bit awkward and uncomfortable at times, especially as the baby grows bigger. After about eight months, the baby starts to move into its final position in the uterus because it's getting ready to be born.

Now I think I've told you enough about life in the uterus, so if you don't mind, we'll go on to talk about birthdays.

Great! I had a brill party for my last birthday! I got a . . .

Hold on a minute! I'm not talking about your *last* birthday. I'm talking about your *first* birthday – the day you were born.

But I can't remember being born – I forget what it was like.

Then I'll remind you about what happens.

Just turn the page.

Five

The First Birthday

After nine months in its mother's womb, the baby is ready to be born. Giving birth to a baby takes time, and both the mother and baby have to work very hard. That's why childbirth is also called **labour**.

I'M GETTING TOO BIG FOR THIS PLACE!

I'D RATHER JUST STAY HERE AND SUCK MY THUMB!

The first thing that happens at childbirth is that the muscles in the mother's tummy begin to tighten and then relax again. This is called **contraction**. ("Contracting" means "getting smaller"). The mother then knows that the baby is ready to come out into the world. At first the contractions may occur every half-hour or so, but they gradually grow more frequent and they become stronger.

These contractions slowly open the **cervix** (neck of the womb). At the same time they reduce the size of the womb, helping to ease the baby downwards. The baby's head now presses against the cervix.

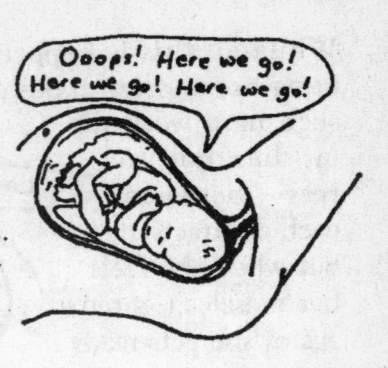

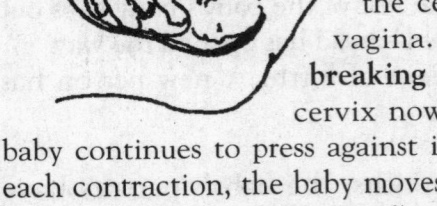

Gradually the pressure becomes too great and the bag of amniotic fluid bursts. The fluid flows through the cervix and down the vagina. This is called the **breaking of the waters.** The cervix now opens fully as the baby continues to press against it. With the help of each contraction, the baby moves through the cervix into the vagina (or **birth canal**).

Normally the vagina is a very narrow opening but the sides of the vagina are made in such a way that they can stretch to allow the baby to pass through, and this is exactly what happens. With each contraction, the baby moves further down the birth canal (vagina) while the womb closes behind it.

While all this is happening, the mother helps by using her muscles to push the baby out. Because it is such hard work the mother has to rest between each contraction, but when she feels her muscles tighten again, she gets ready to push once more. All this pushing is exhausting work and it requires great effort. Contractions can also be painful.

The baby's head usually comes out through the vagina first. Then the rest of the baby's body slips out quite easily as the baby's head has opened the way.

This is the moment of birth. A new person has come into the world.

For nine long months, the baby's parents have been hoping and praying that everything would go well, so you can imagine their joy when they hold their new baby for the very first time.

As your parents once held you.

And that's the story of your first birthday.

What happened to me next?

Well, you were then given the blue treatment:
- the blue babygrow
- the blue cuddly elephant
- the blue dribbler
- the blue everything

But at least, blue is a nice colour. Who'd want pink?

Any more questions?

Loads of them. Are all babies born head first?

You're really testing me today. No, all babies are not born head first. Some babies come out the other way round, feet first. This is called a **breech** birth, and it can be little more difficult for the mother.

And some babies are born by **Caesarean Section**.

This happens when the doctor helps the baby come into the world by a special operation. If the doctor realises that the baby cannot be born naturally, then a Caesarean birth may be necessary. The mother's **abdomen** (tummy) is cut through and the baby is lifted out. After this the mother receives stitches to close the cut. There are many reasons why a Caesarean birth may be necessary. Perhaps it's because the woman's pelvis is too narrow for the baby to pass out, or because the placenta or umbilical cord are in the way.

Incidentally, the word "Caesarean" has nothing to do with the Roman Caesars. It comes from the Latin word "caedere", which means "to cut".

Did you know that there are special names for the doctor and nurse who assist at birth? The doctor, who can be female or male, is called an **obstetrician**, and the nurse is a **midwife**.

Huh! Everyone knows that.

Well, have you any more questions?

Plenty.

How is it some parents have twins?

Why do some twins look alike and others look different?

How come some babies are boys and other babies are girls?

Why are some babies put in incubators?

What is Down syndrome?

Why are some babies born with defects?

Why are . . .

Hey, hold on a minute! Let me answer those one at a time.

You want to know about twins first, right?

Yeah!

Well, there are two types of twins.

First there are **Identical Twins**. They are the same sex and look very alike.

SPOT THE DIFFERENCE

Then there are **Fraternal Twins**. They don't look the same and may be different in sex.

Let's take identical twins first. When a sperm joins with an ovum, the egg is said to be fertilised. If a

fertilised egg splits in half at a very early stage, each half will go on to develop into a separate baby. But because the two babies develop from the same fertilised egg, they will be the same sex and will look alike.

IDENTICAL TWINS:

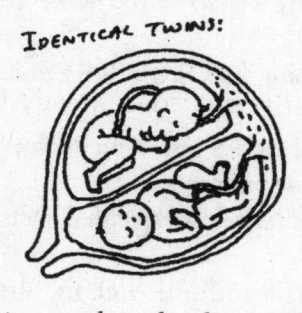

Can identical twins touch each other inside the womb?

Not really. While they are both in the same bag of amniotic fluid, they are separated from each other by a thin wall of cells. They share the same placenta but each has its own umbilical cord.

And what about fraternal twins?

Well, it's different for fraternal twins. Sometimes two ova are released at the same time from a woman's ovaries. If these two eggs are fertilised by two separate sperm from the father, they will be fraternal twins. Can you spot the difference in the illustrations?

FRATERNAL TWINS:

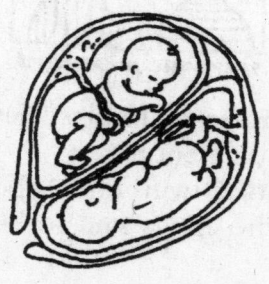

Fraternal twins may look quite different to each other. They may be the same sex (two girls or two boys) or one of each sex (a boy and a girl). Inside the uterus, fraternal twins each have their own placenta and their own separate bag of amniotic fluid.

How are twins born?

In the normal way. First one baby is born. Then, because the birth canal has already been stretched, the other arrives quite quickly. Now, what's your next question?

About babies being either boys or girls. How does that happen?

Do you remember what I told you about the sperm and the ovum?

Sure. The sperm comes from the man and the ovum comes from the woman. When they join together, that's when a baby starts.

Very good. I hope you're always like this in school.

Em . . . well . . . I . . . eh . . .

Don't tell me you're not attentive during Science and Maths!

I'm no good at Maths.

Then you'll really have to listen carefully now because I'm going to do some Maths with you.

Aw! Bo-ring! Skip the Maths. I thought you were going to tell me about the sex of babies.

But I have to do some Maths with you to explain how babies are girls or boys. You remember what a sperm is, don't you?

Yes!

And an ovum?

Of course I do.

OK, I was just checking.

Well, each sperm contains 23 **chromosomes** and each ovum also contains 23 chromosomes. Therefore when the ovum and the sperm meet and join, how many chromosomes are there in total?

Easy. There's 46 chromosomes.

Excellent. This 46 is made up of 23 matching pairs. The chromosomes from the mother and the father match according to the genetic pieces of information they carry. Each chromosome contains thousands of genes which decide your body shape, colour of eyes, hair, and so on. In each matching pair, the stronger or dominant gene wins. That's why children may have their mother's eyes and their grandad's nose. The stronger gene decides.

Ughh! Who'd want your grandad's nose?

Chromosomes also carry instructions about the sex of the baby. These sex chromosomes have been given special names. They're either **X-chromosomes** for making a female baby, or **Y-chromosomes** for making a male baby.

They're BO-RING names. I could make up better ones.

Actually they're called X-chromosomes and Y-chromosomes because, when you look at them under a microscope, they look like an "X" and a "Y".

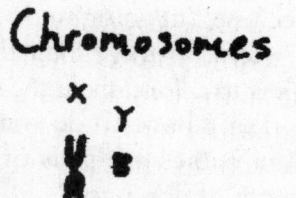

You still have to tell me about Down Syndrome and lots besides.

Anyway, in the ovum from the mother, the sex chromosome is always an X-chromosome.

And in the sperm from the father, the sex chromosome can be either an X-chromosome or a Y-chromosome.

Look, I'll show you.

If the X-chromosome in the ovum meets an X-chromosome in the sperm, the baby will be a girl.

So X + X = a girl.

Exactly. And if the X-chromosome in the ovum meets a Y-chromosome in the sperm, the baby will be a boy.

So X + Y = a boy.

Now you've got it. Because the sex-chromosome from the ovum is always an "X", it is the chromosome from the father's sperm ("X" or "Y") that determines which sex the baby is going to be.

Could I have been a girl?

Only if your father's sperm which joined the ovum had contained an "X" sex chromosome instead of a "Y" sex chromosome.

Gosh! That was close. But you haven't told me everything yet. What happens to the baby after it has been born? What's an incubator and why are babies put in them? And you still have to tell me about Down syndrome, and babies with defects.

Well, I need a cup of tea after all that talking, so I'm going to take a little break. But I know that Cathy has answered all those questions in *Girlfacts*.

If nobody's around, why don't you flip the book over now and sneak a look at what she told the girls. I know she won't mind.

Turn to page 27, but for goodness sake, don't let the girls catch you reading their side of the book. You know how fussy they can be.

And hurry up and come back to me. I have lots more to tell you.

Seven

Puberty - A Time for Change

Phew! You're back.

I was beginning to get worried about you. You've been gone so long that I thought you'd been caught reading the girls' side of the book. Did you find it interesting?

Yeah, it was great.

What do you want to know about now?

Well, I think I've heard enough about babies for the moment. Can we discuss puberty for a while?

Puberty? Ah, that means the time when a person changes from being a child to being an adult. These changes are not just physical. There are also emotional changes . . .

What does "emotional" mean?

Our emotions have to do with how we feel about people and things. Then there are social changes. That means getting on with others. All in all, puberty is a very important time in a person's life.

How long does it last?

Oh, from the age of nine or ten until the late teens for girls, and a bit later for boys. It depends on each individual person.

Why is it different for each person?

The brain controls our growth and development

33

and no growth takes place until the brain is ready. As we are all different, we each have our own individual time-plan to begin puberty.

Imagine for a moment an architect's plan for an apartment block. Although the plan for the whole building is there from the very beginning, it is erected in stages, from the foundations right through to the finishing touches.

Well, it's the same with the human body. As you already know, the plan for our bodies is carried in the . . .?

Chromosomes.

Just checking to see that you haven't nodded off.

You're right, of course. The chromosomes tell what type of person we'll turn out to be. They decide our height, weight, colour of eyes, personality, and so on, and just as architects' plans are all different, so too each person has a different body plan. That's what makes each person a

And people grow quicker during puberty, don't they?

Yes, they do. You see, people don't grow at the same rate all their lives. Puberty is a time when we grow at a faster rate than normal. This quick growing is called a **growth spurt**.

I'm sure you know someone who has suddenly shot up in a short space of time.

Yeah! And girls begin to develop . . . em . . .

Breasts. Look, I'm sure you know many other words for the body parts and most of them are probably slang terms, but I'm going to give you the correct words and you should use them from now on. Okay?

Okay.

Let's begin by taking a closer look at the changes that take place in the body. It all starts with **hormones**. Hormones are chemicals produced by the **endocrine glands** to help our bodies work smoothly. One of these glands, the **pituitary gland**, is in the brain.

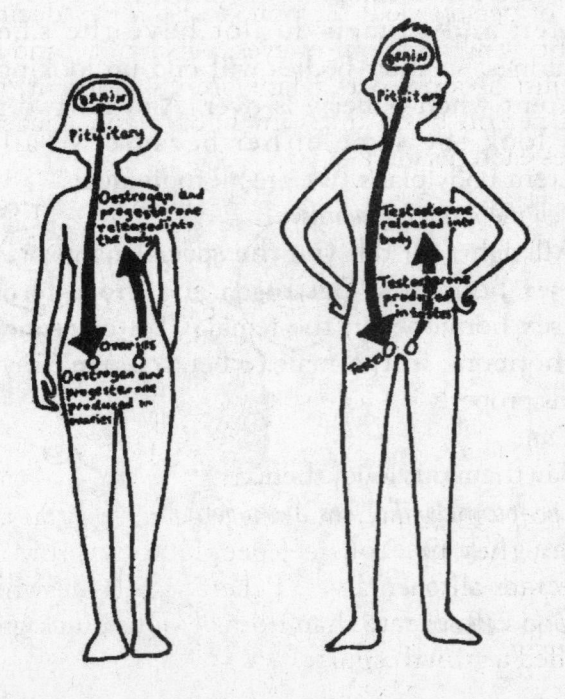

At puberty, the pituitary gland sends out hormones which travel through the bloodstream until they reach the sex glands. In girls, the sex glands are in the ovaries.

That's where the ova are stored.

Correct. And in boys, the sex glands are in the . . .?

Testicles?

Well done.

The sex glands then begin to produce different hormones which, in turn, trigger off all the changes that take place during puberty. These hormones are called sex hormones because they help the testes and the ovaries to develop.

Men and women do not have the same sex hormones, so their bodies will end up looking quite different when puberty is over. And no two people will look the same either because we all have different body plans. We are all individuals.

Tell me more big words.

All right. I'll tell you the special names given to the sex hormones. **Oestrogen** and **Progesterone** are the sex hormones in the female. **Testosterone** is the sex hormone in the male. I bet you can't say those words properly.

Can.

Say them out loud, then.

Oes-(sounds like "ees")-tro-gen.

Pro-ges-te-rone.

Tes-tos-te-rone.

Good effort.

Are you going to tell me about girls as well?

Yes. In fact I'm going to begin with girls. You're not embarrassed, are you?

Who, me? Of course not.

In that case, I'll continue.

These are the biggest changes that happen when girls arrive at the age of puberty:

- They begin to grow taller
- Breasts begin to develop
- Their hips become rounder
- Sweat glands begin to work overtime
- Hair begins to grow under the arms and around the vulva. Do you remember where the vulva is?

I do. It's the name for the female genital area.

Hey, I'm impressed. And now for the biggest change of all:

- Girls begin to have their **periods**. Another name for periods is **Menstruation**. This is a sign that a girl is now old enough to have a baby.

What happens during menstruation?

About every four weeks, a small amount of blood comes out through the vagina. This trickle of blood is called a period.

Actually, if you want to know more about periods, why not read what Cathy has told the girls. But if you know enough for the moment, stay with me, because I'm going to tell you all about what happens to boys during puberty.

It's as well we're still on our own, isn't it? After all, girls might find the information about "how boys develop" a little embarrassing.

Eight

More Changes for Boys

Blame Testosterone.

Yes, the male sex hormone is responsible for all the changes which happen in boys when puberty begins.

Just think of it. You'll look in the mirror one day and there you'll see it.

What?

A spot. The next day, there'll be skillions of them.

Then your voice will start to sound squeaky.

Eeek!

And hair will grow around your private parts.

Oh, no! What will cause all that to happen to me?

That's simple. Puberty.

Let me explain.

The biggest change in boys at puberty is that the

testicles start to grow and develop. They will now have the capacity to produce the special sex cells that are used in making babies.

Not . . . sperm?

Yes, you're right. The answer is sperm.

In theory, these sperm could help to make a baby because sperm fertilise the ovum during intercourse.

But of course, boys of your age are far too young to have the responsibility of making and minding babies. You see, babies need people to be adult in every way in order to mind them and take care of them, and people of your age just aren't ready.

But I don't feel anything happening to me.

Making sperm happens without you even realising it because it happens inside your body.

Did you know that the adult male manufactures about 5000 sperm per second?

Girls couldn't do that.

You will also start to grow taller. But remember that everybody has their own special time for beginning their growth spurt. Some boys get fed up waiting to start growing. They feel really small when their friends shoot up and they're left behind. Others feel self-conscious when they're suddenly twenty metres taller than their friends and get slagged about their height. There's nothing you can do at times like that except be patient. It generally works out well in the end.

Your penis and testicles become larger. Before puberty, the penis is used only to pass urine (or pee). After puberty, your penis has two functions: to pee with and also to pass semen. This is the liquid which . . .

Contains sperm. I remember. But is it possible to . . .

No, of course not. You can't pee and pass semen at the same time. It's a total impossibility.

Then how does the semen pass out?

That's easy. Your penis will become hard at times. This is called an **erection.** The penis is like a kind of sponge. When blood rushes into the penis, it becomes stiff and stands out from the body. This may cause you some embarrassment at times, but there's no need to worry as nobody else will notice. Anyway, it will probably happen to you when you're warm in bed. Sometimes semen will come out of your penis when you're asleep. This is called a **nocturnal emission** or a **"wet dream."** You will probably be having a romantic dream about girls when it happens. No need to worry. All this is quite normal. Just keep a towel or roll of toilet paper handy in case you need to wipe the sheets.

Pubic hair begins to grow. Pubic hair is the hair which grows around your genital area.

Hair will begin to grow on your face and upper lip. This will start at around fourteen years of age or a little later. You will then have to begin shaving. Use shaving foam or shaving gel as your skin will be tender. Ask your father or older brother for advice about razor blades.

There's no point in asking my brother about blades. He always cuts himself shaving.

That reminds me. When you start to shave, don't use anybody else's razor blade. Razor blades, like toothbrushes, are personal things which should never be shared. Now, where was I?

You were talking about hair starting to grow.

Oh, yes. You'll also notice that hair will begin to grow in your armpits, and possibly even on your chest and legs. And, of course, your face will alter shape.

What?

It's true. This happens mostly because your jaw drops, making your face longer.

But I like my face the way it is.

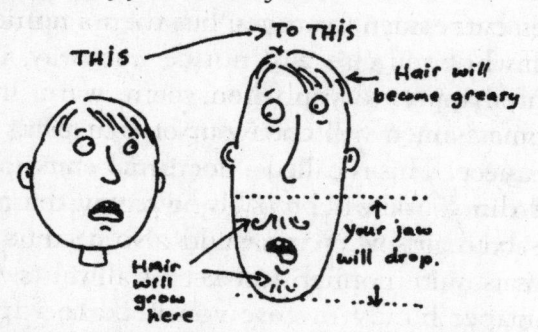

THIS → TO THIS

Hair will become greasy

Hair will grow here

your jaw will drop.

Your **voice will break**. This means that you'll develop a deeper voice. Ignore the squeakiness. That only lasts for a short while.

I wonder what I'll sound like after my voice changes?

Your shoulders and chest will broaden and you'll become more muscular.

Oh, great, then all the girls will admire me.

Then you'll have to start taking better care of how you look. How often do you clean yourself?

Regularly.

Yes, once every month, whether you need to or not.

It's never that long.

Well, you'll have to wash more often now because the sweat glands on your skin will work overtime during puberty. Sweating is natural. Even when your

body is at normal temperature, you sweat. Actually sweat helps by ridding your body of waste through the pores in your skin.

So you see now why you need to wash yourself well every day. Take frequent showers – they're very refreshing – and keep your hair clean. When you wash your face and hands, don't forget to clean your nails. And while I'm at it, brush your teeth a couple of times every day. Then you'll have something to show off when you smile.

No, not your toothbrush. Your teeth.

You sound like my mother. Next you'll be telling me to change my socks.

How did you know I was going to say that? And not just your socks. You should also change your underwear every day. Remember that all this sweat is going into your clothes so you must change daily to be really clean.

But that means my mother will have to do extra washing and ironing.

Oh, no it doesn't. It means that YOU will have to learn how to use the washing machine and then hang things out to dry. It's time for you to learn to be more independent. You can start by collecting all of the dirty socks that you kick out of sight under the bed and put them in the washing machine. Then I'll show you how the washing machine works.

I don't suppose you'd believe me if I said that I am allergic to being clean. No, I didn't think so. Okay, show me how to use the washing machine.

Good. Then we can go on to talk about something else.

Nine
Friends

Let's talk about friends for a change. Have you any?

Oh, sure, lots of them.

Do you ever fall out with them?

Of course not.

What about last week when you broke Patrick Hanley's ruler?

But that was an accident. Anyway, he called me a name.

Then it wasn't an accident.

Well, it nearly was. I just meant to bend it.

Did you apologise?

Yeah. The teacher told me to, and I had to buy him a new one.

And now you're friends again?

Yeah.

Well, that shows you that you can't just do what you like and not expect other people to be upset at times. People have feelings, and those feelings can be easily hurt. Do you ever think about what friends are for?

Yeah. For buying sweets when you've no money yourself. Ha! Ha!

Very funny. Seriously though, are you a good friend to others?

Em . . . let me think now . . .

I'm sure you know what it takes to be a good friend, but do you try to behave like one? You've been learning for years now how to be kind and considerate, how to give and take, how to share and be generous.

But it's impossible to like everybody all the time.

True, it isn't easy at times. When others aren't being nice to you, it's really difficult to be nice to them.

Perhaps they're just having a bad day or are worried about something. In that case, you could ask them what's wrong or you could try to distract them, or tell a joke.

But if they're just being rotten towards you and you can't do anything about it, then you should move away from them.

But you can't move away from your family. You're stuck with them.

And they're stuck with you.

Sometimes brothers and sisters can annoy and tease you and drive you mad. But you probably get on their nerves too, you know, when you lose your temper with them, or try to get them into trouble or hurt them.

Me! Never.

Pardon?

Well, we just have teeny-weeny, teenchy little arguments.

That happens in most families. But it's worth making the effort to get on with them. After all, you share so much with them – your parents, your home, even your room, perhaps? When things go wrong every now and then, you should be able to make up

and forget about it. What should you say when you've caused a row?

Suh . . . Suh . . . Suh . . .

Oh, for goodness sake, the word is "sorry".

But it's hard to say.

I know, but it's a sign that you are becoming mature. You're showing that you realise that you've made a mistake and are sorry for it. Everyone makes a mistake at some stage. When that happens, we should be willing to apologise and to do what we can to make up. Have you a girlfriend?

Was that a knock at the door just now?

Don't try to change the subject. I want to talk about girlfriends for a few minutes. Maybe when you're older, you might want to go out on date.

Me? With a girl?

Well, it's nice to have a special friend and to show that friend that you like her a lot. But even on dates, young people still have to behave. There are rules about sex just the same as there are rules about crossing the road. Kissing and all that may be very nice but sometimes young people may go too far because they don't know when to stop or how to stop.

In a relationship, people should have respect for each other and be able to look out for each other. If one person puts pressure on the other by making them do something they don't want to, then the relationship isn't working anymore. Caring and sharing help to make a relationship work – selfishness and jealousy destroy a relationship. Boys and girls also have to learn how to solve their problems through talking. You can't expect to get your own way all the

time, so every now and then you'll have to give in.

And girls have a right to say "no" just as boys have.

By the way, what are you supposed to say when you make a mistake?

"Sorry."

What about the other little useful words?

What other little words?

"Please" and "thank you".

Oh, those.

Yes, there's nothing wrong with having manners. You like it when people are nice to you, so you should be polite to others. Manners cost nothing and people will respect you for being polite. That's one way of showing you're growing in maturity as well as developing physically.

Sorry! Please! Thank you!

Sorry! Please! Thank you!

Sorry! Please! Thank you!

What are you doing?

Just practising.

Good. You need to.

Ten
Bad Words

Do you ever say bad words?

No.

I think you do.

They might just slip out – I don't usually say bad words.

When you were about one year old, you learned words like "Ma-Ma", "Da-Da", "ball" and "dog". At around two years, you were able to say things like "All gone", "Want more" and "Where Teddy?" You've learned lots more since then. You can use words to describe things, to say what you like and dislike, and to share your ideas or information. Words also allow you to talk about your feelings and your actions. We use words every day of our lives when we talk to other people, or when we read or write. Without words, it would be much more difficult for us to communicate with other people. Although there are other ways of communicating, people mostly do it by using words. We're using words at the moment to communicate. Some of these words have to do with sex, including, for example, penis, vagina, testicles, ovaries, sperm, ovum, breasts, erection, wet dreams and sexual intercourse.

These are the correct words to use when talking about sex.

Some people think that sex-type words are naughty or wrong but they're not. When we use sex-words in the right way, that's okay. For example, I'm using sex-words the right way when I explain them to you.

It's also okay to use sex-words and bad words if you're asking your mother or father or teacher what they mean. But words can be used the wrong way too, and lots of these words have to do with sex, haven't they? They're rude names for the private parts of the body or for sexual activity. Some of these terms are very nasty.

Well, all the other boys use bad words. And grown-ups use them too.

True. And it's not very fair on you when they do that. But remember, just because you hear a word, it doesn't mean you have to go out and say it yourself.

But sometimes I think it's cool to use bad words.

And it also becomes a habit. Besides, swear words do not help people to communicate very well. In fact, if we only said swear words to each other, there'd be very little real conversation in the world. Using swear words is a bad habit to get into. Words can also be used to bully others. It happens all the time.

It happened to me once.

But you don't have to put up with it. If someone is calling you slang names, or saying nasty things about you or your parents, or using bad language at you, then you must tell someone about it. Words can hurt just as much as hitting or kicking. It's just that the hurt is on the inside so nobody may know about it unless you tell.

You've heard people say:

"Sticks and stones can break my bones . . ."

". . . But names will never hurt me . . . "

Everyone knows that rhyme.

But it's not true, is it? Words can hurt.

But if a bad word just . . . pops out by accident?

If you bang your thumb with a hammer, or if you get a sudden fright, a bad word might just suddenly just pop out. But you really should be very careful about using bad language towards other people or with other people. You might think it's cool now for a while, but believe me, most people don't like it one little bit. And most girls don't like it, either.

Who cares about girls? All of my friends are boys.

Oh no, they're not. I know who your girlfriend is.

What? How did you find out?

Aha, then I'm right! You do have a girlfriend.

AURGGH! Me and my big mouth.

Yes, and I hope you watch what that big mouth says from now on. It's a good idea to think first and speak second.

Eleven

Drugfacts

You've made a mistake.

Yes. I know. It's called a deliberate error. Of course I know it should be "Drug Facts" – two separate words – instead of "Drugfacts". It just looks sort of . . . smart, don't you think?

Whenever I make deliberate errors in school, my teacher always points them out to me. She says I can learn from my mistakes.

Learning from mistakes is a good way to learn. I don't mean just in school. I'm talking about everything to do with life. When we make small mistakes, it's easy to correct them and put them right. If, for example, you had a row with your best friend, or if you told lies, you can apologise and put things right.

What about serious mistakes?

Ah, they can be harder to fix. Serious mistakes cause people to get hurt, sometimes pretty badly. Take road accidents, for example. When drivers make mistakes, the consequences can be serious. Vehicles can be damaged or written-off and people can end up in hospital. Worse still, some road accidents cause deaths.

People die from drugs too.

Yes. Some people are addicted to drugs such as

heroin and cocaine. Of course, when they were your age, they probably didn't take those drugs.

So what happened to them?

It's very hard to say. Each person has a different reason. Then when they're hooked or addicted, it's often too late for them to come off drugs, no matter how hard they try. Because this craving for drugs is overwhelming, an addict needs great courage and determination in order to stop.

I've never seen any drugs.

Oh yes, you have. Tobacco and alcohol are drugs, but they are legal. However, they can only be sold under certain conditions. For example, people have to be over a certain age before they can be allowed to buy them.

In other words, there are rules to be obeyed, and when people are caught breaking those rules, they will be punished.

What's wrong with drugs?

Absolutely nothing. Many drugs are manufactured to help people who are sick or in pain. These are called **medicines**, and of course, all medicines should only be taken according to the instructions.

I never think of medicines as drugs . . .

But they are. Medicines contain drugs which are designed to help people. Other drugs are manufactured for enjoyment, such as alcohol and tobacco. Many people enjoy a drink or a smoke. Some enjoy both.

However, drugs have **side-effects**. That means that as well as easing pain and headaches, or making people feel relaxed, they have other effects and not all of these are good. Let's take alcohol as an example.

While many adults enjoy a drink, the alcohol quickly begins to affect their judgement, feelings and behaviour. That's why we have a **drink-drive alcohol limit**. Alcohol affects a person's ability to drive well, because driving involves good judgement and quick reactions, and the more alcohol a person takes, the less capable he or she is of thinking straight. So if people choose to take alcohol, they must obey the rules in order to keep themselves and others safe and the best rule is **"DON'T EVER DRINK AND DRIVE."** Actually, that's what growing up is all about – being able to make good choices.

Is alcohol a bad drug, then?

No. For many adults, drinking alcohol in moderation is sensible and enjoyable. But taking alcohol in excess can be very harmful. A person who is addicted to alcohol is called an **alcoholic.** When people are drunk, they have little or no control over their minds or their behaviour. That's why drunk people often say and do things that they would never say or do when they are sober.

I know that smoking has a bad effect on your lungs.

And that's not all. The more people smoke, the more likely they are to suffer from cancer, bronchitis, strokes, blood clots, heart disease, phlegmy coughs and bad circulation.

Ugh!

And their clothes and hair will smell.

Ugghh!

And they'll have bad breath.

Eewww!?

Did you ever hear of passive smoking?

No . . .

That's when a non-smoker . . .

That's me.

. . . breathes in somebody else's smoke.

You mean that if I'm in a room with someone who's smoking, and I breathe in their smoke, I'm a passive smoker?

Exactly. That's what passive smoking is. And passive smoking can be very harmful. That's why smoking is banned in many places today.

I've heard that smoking can have an effect on a baby in the womb. Is that true?

Yes, smoking affects the general health of the mother, and babies need mothers to be as healthy as possible. Smoking also can reduce the amount of **oxygen** available to the baby in the womb. The baby may be smaller in size, and may be born prematurely. By the way, alcohol and other drugs can also affect the baby in the womb, so expectant mothers have to be very careful about smoking and taking alcohol or other harmful drugs.

I think everybody should be careful about smoking and taking alcohol.

D'you know, sometimes you say very sensible things. Have you any more questions?

Yes. Where do people get these other drugs such as ecstasy and cocaine?

Because these drugs are illegal, they have to be bought from dealers. These are people who sell illegal drugs in places where they can't be seen doing it. Some of these dealers even try to sell drugs to small children now so that they can get them addicted

early. They offer them drugs that look like sweets, hoping that kids won't know the difference.

That's never happened to me.

Maybe not, but someday, somebody may offer you drugs, perhaps just to try them. It may even be somebody you know in school. Don't be surprised if that happens. You may be put under pressure to experiment but you'll have to be prepared for that. Have your answer ready beforehand and stick to it.

But drugs cost a lot of money.

Of course drugs are very expensive and so many people have to steal or commit other crimes to pay for them.

Some people die from taking drugs, don't they?

Yes, that's true. Drugs contain very powerful chemicals which the human body is just not designed to cope with. So if a person takes a drug overdose, that is, more than their body can cope with, they may well die before they receive medical help. That's because the drugs are often taken when there are no other people around who can help.

What's solvent abuse?

Solvent abuse is when people inhale (sniff or breathe in) the fumes from glues, gases and sprays in aerosols, for instance. These solvents also contain chemicals which are very dangerous. Unfortunately, many young people don't find out about the effects of drugs and solvents until after they have taken them. This means that experimenting with drugs and solvents is very risky behaviour, and should be utterly avoided.

Some people say that drugs will make you feel

good, but they will always leave you tired and depressed when they have stopped working. Also, some drugs are injected into the body. If people share needles (syringes), they are at risk of becoming infected with certain viruses such as HIV, or of catching Hepatitis, because their blood comes into contact with infected blood.

What's a virus?

A **virus** is an organism much smaller than a bacteria. Because it's so small it can pass through filters that will keep out bacteria. Viruses only live in plants and animals that are themselves alive. They spread in the same way as bacteria. When conditions are right, they can multiply rapidly and cause great harm. Diseases such as polio and smallpox are caused by a virus. So too are influenza – the flu – and the common cold.

And AIDS?

Yes, AIDS is caused by a virus. It's called HIV. V stands for Virus. If a person is carrying the virus, they are said to be HIV Positive. HIV carriers can pass on the virus to another person. That's why people are being told to practice safe sex, so that they won't be infected with the AIDS virus or any other kind of sexual disease.

What are STDs?

The letters STD stand for Sexually Transmitted Disease. They are sometimes called STI's "Sexually Transmitted Infections". These are diseases passed from one person to another mostly by sexual contact – that means the virus can pass during sexual intercourse. It's very easy for a virus to pass in this way. Sometimes a

person can be carrying a virus but you would not know. That's whay people have to be very careful when it comes to having sex.

Antibiotics are chemicals actually made from bacteria. They help the body to recover from many illnesses by killing the bacteria without harming the body. However, there is no cure yet for the AIDS virus but some drugs can help.

Hey! I've an idea. Why not do one of your warnings like at the beginning of the book? That way the message will be clear to everybody.

That's an excellent suggestion.

Warning

Drugs and solvents are dangerous

Drugs and solvents can kill

Make your body a drug-free zone

Say "no" to smoking and alcohol

Get a life and keep it!

Psst! I like the last line.

A Few Final Words

Is that all there is to know about growing up?

No, but I've told you as much as you need to know for now.

But I've enjoyed our chats. Can't we talk for another while? I'm sure I could come up with more questions.

Here's one for you? How many teeth has a . . .?

47!

Rhinoceros?

Aw, I thought you were going to say mosquito again. I don't know how many teeth a rhinoceros has.

Nor do I, but I do know that as you get older it's not enough just to know things. You have to be able to use the information you have to make good decisions for yourself and for others. That's why I've explained so many things for you. You can read this book again, if you wish, to make sure you understand everything.

What'll I do now?

Oh, you could tidy your room or do some extra homework. Did you take the dog for his walk yet? Does the chimney need cleaning?

That's not what I had in mind. Do you think that I could . . .

What?

You know?

Oh, all right. Turn the book over now and start again at the other side. Don't mind what the girls say. I'm sure they don't mean a word of it. I enjoyed reading *Girlfacts* myself so I'm sure you will too.

See you later.

BOY

IT'S OK to flip over now.